PORTRAIT *of an*
IMMIGRANT

*The Odyssey of a Slovak Boy -
who Immigrated to America
with his Family in 1939*

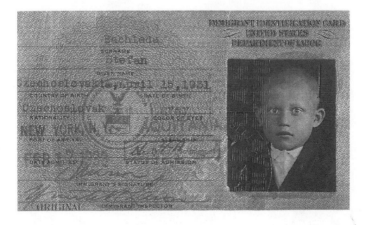

STEVEN A BACHLEDA

ISBN: 1491013117
ISBN-13: 9781491013113

Library of Congress Control Number: 2013912987
CreateSpace Independent Publishing Platform
North Charleston, South Carolina

Dedicated to my Beloved Mother

Mary Bachleda

TABLE OF CONTENTS

PROLOGUE vii

CHAPTER 1: The Very Beginning 1

CHAPTER 2: My Early Years in Czechoslovakia 11

CHAPTER 3: The Journey to America 31

CHAPTER 4: Our New Beginning in America...................... 45

CHAPTER 5: The War Years 61

CHAPTER 6: Our Family Grows and Changes 91

CHAPTER 7: Years of Joy and Sorrow 111

CHAPTER 8: Realizing the American Dream 135

CHAPTER 9: The Later Years 149

EPILOGUE...167

REFERENCES 169

PROLOGUE

Several years ago, I contacted my local newspaper, the North Haven Citizen, and I told them that I had a human-interest story, which I would like to share about my family. They proceeded to interview me, and an article was published in May of 2009, entitled 'Patriotism and Struggle for Survival: One North Haven Veteran's Story.' After publication, I received a number of phone calls from people, who knew me. They told me, that they thought it was a wonderful story, and then went on to say, it would make a great book. I had been thinking about writing my story for the longest time, but kept putting it off. The feedback from the newspaper article gave me the incentive to sit down and start writing.

I think most of us have wondered about our family history, yet few of us actually have the privilege of knowing much about our ancestors. Often, I have been curious about where my family came from, who my ancestors were, what they were like, and what kind of lives did they lead. Therefore, the main reason that I'm writing this book is as a legacy to my descendants. I hope my story will give future generations a past, which they can reflect upon long after I'm gone.

I realize that our lives, while we were growing up were very different, compared to today's average American family. I also know that, no matter how much I try to describe what life was like during those dark and uncertain times, it will be very difficult for present and future generations to fully understand. However, I hope our experiences in life can help, guide, or inspire them in some way.

Chapter 1:

THE VERY BEGINNING

My Parents

My parents were born in a picturesque farming town called Zdiar, situated at the base of the High Tatra Mountain Range bordering Poland, which was then known as Czechoslovakia, but today is called Slovakia. The town, at that time, had a population of about five hundred people. It was surrounded

by large stretches of woods on the mountain slopes. There were also numerous small ponds and brooks. All the homes there were constructed of wood and stucco. They had steep tin roofs as the area would get huge amounts of snow in the winter months, and this type of roof allowed the snow to slide right off. None of the homes had electricity or basements. There was also no indoor plumbing, so water was drawn from the well that each home had. Outhouses were used. The town was very popular with tourists, who came to visit because of the mountains, where people skied in the winter and hiked in the summer.

My father, Anton Bachleda, was born in 1896. He was the eldest of his siblings. He had four brothers: Frantisek, Jan, Stefan, and Pavel. In addition, he had three sisters: Veronika, Maria, and Ruzena. He was tall, standing about six-feet two, solidly built, with thick light-brown hair, grey eyes, and a ruddy complexion. It was very typical for farmers to have large families, in those days, to help with the numerous farming chores.

Originally, my father's father came from Poland, more than likely from a city called Krakow, where a number of Bachledas are still living. A New York newspaper photo from the funeral of Pope John Paul II (who was from southern Poland) showed a woman dressed in traditional Polish attire carrying a placard, which mentioned that the Bachledas were his relatives.

Apparently, while growing up, my father and his brothers were a rowdy bunch, always fighting and getting into trouble, so much so, it was said that their mother didn't allow them to wear suspenders or belts to hold up their pants. If they had to hold their pants up with one arm, it limited them from fighting. I'm not sure how true that was, but it definitely got the point across about their behavior. Whenever there was trouble in town, it seemed, the Bachleda brothers were always involved.

The men in the town spent much of their time in the local drinking parlors, especially in the winter, when there were not as many farming chores to be done. They drank and socialized, coming home late in the evening. Of course, in addition to that, they all had their own homemade vodka, which they consumed quite often. Many struggled with alcoholism, including my father.

As a young man, my father and his brothers went into the business of buying and selling horses. They traveled over the High Tatra Mountains into Poland and bought horses from the Polish farmers at very reasonable prices. The horses were smuggled back home, late at night through the mountain passes in the Tatras, in order to avoid having to pay tariffs. Once they were back in Czechoslovakia, they sold the horses to farmers at a very good profit. After doing that for several years, along with other business ventures, my father had accumulated quite a bit of money. Therefore, he decided it was time to get married. He always had his sights set on my mother.

My mother, Maria Oleksakova, was born in 1898, and she was also the oldest of her siblings. She had two sisters and four brothers. Her sisters were Agata and Ruzena, and her brothers were Anton, Josef, Valent, and Gustin. Since she was the oldest, my mother worked in the fields and tended to the farm, along with her father doing the work of a man. She was also expected to help her mother in the care of her siblings. In later years, she was diagnosed with a weak heart, due to the great amount of strenuous duties that she was required to perform during all those early years.

My mother was considered to be one of the prettiest girls in town, so after coming of age, she had a number of suitors. She was about five-feet five inches tall with a beautiful complexion, natural rose-colored cheeks, light-brown hair, and soft grey-blue eyes, which reflected her kind and loving personality. There was one boy in the town, she had known for years and hoped to marry someday. However, he was very poor and came from a very large family. My mother's parents didn't approve of him, because they felt that he wouldn't be able to provide a good living for their daughter.

Courtship, Marriage, and Children

When my father started to court my mother, he and his brothers pretty much scared off all the other suitors, except for the young man, whom she was in love with. However, her parents were strongly encouraging her to marry my father as he was more successful. My mother also felt that her parents were intimidated by my father.

In those days, you really didn't have much choice once your parents decided whom you should marry. With constant urging from her parents, my mother reluctantly accepted my father's proposal. When my mother's favorite suitor learned that my mother had agreed to marry my father, he was crushed, telling my mother that he loved her dearly. He begged her to please reconsider as they were both brokenhearted.

My mother said that she was always fearful of my father, but in the end she gave in to her parent's wishes and married him, despite having serious doubts about whether or not she had made the right decision. As it turned out, she regretted that decision for the rest of her life.

They were married in 1918, at the quaint little Catholic Church in Zdiar. My parents also settled there and lived in a duplex house, which my father and his brother, Stefan, had built. My parents resided there for several years, and during that time my mother gave birth to their first four children. Their first child was my brother, John (Jan), born in 1920. The next child was a baby girl named Sophia, but she passed away several months after she

was born, due to some sort of illness. Then my mother gave birth to Tony (Anton) in 1923 and Ronnie (Veronika) in 1925.

The Move to Trstany and More Children

In 1926, my father decided to invest his funds. With the help of financing from the bank, he purchased large tracts of farmland and also a large house in a village called Trstany, which was about forty-eight miles south of Zdiar. The village consisted of about ten families. It was nestled in a little valley, surrounded by numerous stretches of lush woods and forests, with other small villages a few miles away.

The house my father bought had once been owned by a wealthy family, who owned a small factory in the village, which employed a number of people. Inside the house there were several beautiful murals painted on the high ceilings and the walls of all the rooms. On one particular wall there was a beautiful scene depicting the mountains and the valleys of the surrounding area. Another wall had scenes from the life of Jesus and the Virgin Mary, along with the Apostles. Apparently, the previous family had been forced to close their factory and sold their home because of financial difficulties.

The weather in Trstany was about the same as northern New England in the United States, with cold, snowy winters, and pleasant summers with cool breezes from the nearby mountains. In the frigid winters, the moose and bears came out from the deep woods into the village, searching for food. There was always plenty of wild game in the forests, but you were forbidden to hunt or trap them as the state owned all the forestland. There were times when a deer or wild boar would stray onto your farmland, and it was only then, you had the right to kill it. The farmers had root cellars where they stored their fresh foods to keep them from spoiling. They also had smoke rooms, which was where they cured and stored various meats.

The house my father bought had a large attic, which was used as a smoke room to cure meats, sausages, and bacon. There was a thick layer of sand on the floor of the attic, which was put there in case of a fire in the house below. Supposedly, the intent was, if the ceiling of the first floor burned, the ceiling would then collapse, and the sand would help to extinguish the fire below.

Shortly after taking ownership of the house, my father discovered a large wooden cross buried in the sand on the floor of the attic. No one seemed to know the reason as to why it was buried there. My father had the cross removed from the attic. Upon learning of the buried cross my mother, a devout Catholic, sent for a priest to bless the house because being superstitious, she thought, it was a bad omen. My father decided to donate the cross to the church, and subsequently it was placed in a chapel, which my father had built overlooking the village. Years later, the chapel was rebuilt into a church.

After moving to Trstany, my mother had two more children. Rose (Ruzena) was born in 1927, and Mary (Maria) was born in 1929.

The first few years after our family moved to Trstany, everything went along fine. My mother now had five children, along with domestic help to assist her in maintaining the household. Farm workers were hired by my father to cultivate the large tracts of land that he had purchased. My father owned livestock, and he also had a large stable of horses, along with two beautiful carriages. His stable hands drove him around the towns and villages on various errands. In addition, he owned sheep, which provided wool and milk, from which cheese was made.

Our Father Leaves for America

As the years rolled by, my father started to grow lax, and he became distracted from managing his properties, due to his drinking and womanizing. There was also a world economic Depression on the horizon, and the farm was not earning enough income to repay the bank for the money, which my father had borrowed.

Before long, my father was delinquent in his payments to the bank. Then bit-by-bit, he started to forfeit a number of his properties. As time went on, he could no longer afford to employ his farm workers. He had accumulated huge debts that he owed to the bank, which most likely he would never be able to repay. Soon, the bank confiscated most of the land my father owned, and he was also forced to sell off most of the livestock. We were just left with the house, the furniture, one barn, three cows, pigs, rabbits, geese, ducks, chickens, and a couple of fields. Faced with the threat of going to debtor's prison, he wrote to his brother, Frantisek, who some years earlier had immigrated to America. He had settled in Westfield, Massachusetts, where there was a large Slovak community. Frantisek was doing well financially. My father explained to his brother, Frantisek, the terrible financial situation that he was in and asked him for help.

Frantisek advised him to come to America. He said that he would sponsor him and help him find employment. Then once he earned enough money, he would be able to return back to Czechoslovakia and repay his debts. Therefore, in the fall of 1930, my father bid my mother, who was pregnant with me at the time, farewell, and then he left for America. My mother was left with the responsibility of raising five children and another one soon to be born. She was on her own, with no one to help her. She didn't know for certain if my father would ever return, or if he would just leave us there. In addition, my mother was left with the large debt owed to the bank, which my father was supposed to repay.

Since Ellis Island was no longer used to process immigrants, my father's ship docked directly at the Pier in New York City. His brother, Frantisek, was waiting for him and drove him to his home in Westfield, Massachusetts. My father wrote to my mother, notifying her, that he had arrived safely and started to look for employment.

As fate would have it, when my father reached America the Depression was in full bloom, and there were no jobs to be had. He spent some time with his brother in Massachusetts, but was unable to find a job. Then he decided to look elsewhere, so he went to New York. He settled in a town called Hastings-on-the-Hudson, which had a large Slovak population. Eventually, he was able to find a job at the Anaconda Wire and Cable Company as a factory worker. He then wrote to our mother, saying that soon he would be sending her money regularly. However, when he did send money, he hardly sent anything at all.

My Birth

I, Steven (Stefan) was born in 1931, five months after my father had left for America. In those days babies were born at home, and a midwife would assist with the delivery. All of us were born healthy and were breast fed. Ronnie remembers the day when I was born. She said all the children were outside playing, when they were called into my mother's room to meet me. My mother was in bed, and she looked very happy with a big smile on her face. She was embracing a small bundle, so everyone approached her to see what she was holding. It was then, that they were introduced to the newest member of their family, a brother. I was passed around to each of my siblings, to kiss and welcome me into the family as that was the Slovak tradition.

Chapter 2:

MY EARLY YEARS IN CZECHOSLOVAKIA

Day-to-Day Life

A short time after my father had left for America, the youngest of my mother's four brothers, Gustin, came to live with us. Uncle Gustin had the same loving heart and compassion that my mother possessed. He realized that our mother was having great difficulty, in caring for the farm and raising six young children at the same time. Thankfully, he was there to help. I don't know how, we would have survived without him.

We remained in the big house, which we still owned, along with the barn. We also had a couple of fields that we used for planting a large portion of potatoes and other crops. Fortunately, we were left with three cows, which provided the milk to make butter, along with some pigs, geese, ducks, rabbits, and chickens. There were apple, plum, and pear trees on some of our property. In addition, we had a large garden where we grew carrots, peas, onions, cucumbers, squash, cabbage, turnips, lettuce, and various herbs for seasoning.

Every so often, my mother and Gustin would go to the nearby city of Kezmarek with the help of a neighbor, who had a horse and wagon. They were able to earn some money by selling butter, eggs, fruit, and produce from our fields and garden. While in Kezmarek, my mother purchased cooking supplies such as sugar, salt, flour, and other necessities.

Potatoes and cabbage were our main staples. I remember always eating a lot of potato bread and soup made with potatoes, cabbage, and little bits of bacon. Sometimes for dinner my mother fried bacon, and then she fried potatoes in the bacon fat until they were golden brown, and served them with the chopped bacon. Other times she made chopped cabbage fried in butter, served over homemade noodles. We drank a large glass of buttermilk with most of our meals as it was quite filling.

One of my favorite meals was called Kulasa. Potatoes were boiled until they were very well done, drained, but some of the water was saved. Milk and flour were then added to the potatoes in the pan and beaten until it became a thick paste. The thick paste was put into a large bowl, and mashed on the sides of the bowl, adding some melted butter in the center. Our mother put the bowl in the center of the kitchen table, and we all ate from it, each of us dipping a spoonful of kulasa into the puddle of butter. I was raised on that dish. Of course, there were always the pierogies, dumplings filled with mashed potatoes and cheese, along with all kinds of different fillings, which we always enjoyed.

There was a soup, my mother made called Krupi. It was a thick and hearty barley soup, with bits of ham, carrots, onions, and potatoes. Sometimes for breakfast, we ate scrambled goose eggs as they were very large, and they went a long way toward feeding all of us.

I remember going into the nearby woods with my sisters and our mother to pick wild berries, I especially liked gooseberries. While there, we gathered kindling wood for the stove and searched for wild mushrooms.

At a certain time of year, there were large patches of beautiful red poppies, which grew in the unattended fields. We went into the fields to gather them up, carefully picking out the poppy seeds from the center of the flower, putting them in a pail, and brought them home to our mother. She would grind them up and use them in various cookies and cakes that she baked. There were beautiful rose and lilac bushes surrounding our house, which we picked for our mother when they were in bloom. My mother especially loved lilacs.

Whenever we were sick, our mother treated us with home remedies made from the various herbs, plants, and roots, which came from either the garden or the woods. There were times, when we developed painful boils. Then our mother went out into the woods, returning with some particular kind of large leaves. She applied them to the boil and tied a cloth to keep them in place. After a few days, the boil was gone. If we had any sort of stomach ailment or flu symptoms, our mother dug up a certain type of root in the woods. She put the root in a bottle of whiskey, let it sit there for a few days, and then it was ready to be taken. Then we took a large spoonful of the whiskey, which had a very bitter taste. Usually, we were cured. If we sprained an ankle, we urinated on a cloth, and then we applied it to the area as it reduced the swelling. In a few days, the ankle would feel better.

When we weren't helping our mother with the farm, we played with the neighboring kids. As the youngest, I always tagged along with my sisters and their friends. Everyone was poor, so we had a lot in common. No one had toys, but we found things to play with and had a good time. We made marbles out of clay by putting them out in the sun until they got hard. Other times we carved flutes from tree branches.

There were certain trees, which we were able to pick the sap from, and then we chewed it like gum. The only time, I ever tasted real gum was when a stranger, who was visiting someone in our village gave all of us kids some store-bought gum. I chewed that gum for days and days, putting it on the bedpost when I went to bed.

At times, we would go into the woods and explore, walking through the tall pine trees and treading on the blanket of soft pine needles with our bare feet. I always had a fascination with the woods surrounding our village. To me, they always seemed mysterious and magical. One thing that was so different back then was, when there was a full moon at night it was so bright and clear that it was almost like daytime. That was probably because there was hardly any air pollution.

In the summertime, we never wore shoes, and I remember always stubbing my big toe on the dirt roads. There was a little brook running through the center of our village and out into the open fields. We liked to soak our feet in it and play with the frogs, tadpoles, and the little fish. We also watched the storks, which were nesting and feeding there.

Our baths were taken in a very large metal wash basin, filled with warm water, which had been heated in buckets on the stove. Usually, we bathed only once a week. During the night, we had a chamber pot, which everyone used. We all took turns emptying it in the outhouse when we awoke the next morning.

Being the youngest of six children, I was somewhat sheltered. I didn't realize all of the hardships and worries, which my mother and older siblings had to deal with. My recollection is that growing up in the village of Trstany was one of the happiest times of my life. I loved being with my siblings and our loving mother. I didn't have a worry in the world.

School Days

Our village originally didn't have a schoolhouse of its own. The children walked to the nearest village to attend school there. Since our house was very large, my father allowed the people of the village to use one of the rooms in our house as a classroom for their children. Later, he had a one-room schoolhouse built on one of his properties, which all the children of the village could attend.

The schoolhouse had a pot belly stove to warm us in the winter, an outhouse, and a well. Children of all ages were together in the same room. All the lessons, which we were taught would depend upon age, and we were seated accordingly in the classroom. The village priest was the only teacher for all the children. Everyone was given homework with the emphasis on reading and writing. We were also taught religious studies to prepare us for our First Communion and Confirmation.

I remember one snowy day in the winter when I had arrived at school, and I forgot to brush off the snow from my shoes. The snow on them had melted and left a big puddle of water beneath my feet. When the priest saw it, he didn't ask me about it, instead, he just assumed that I had wet my pants. Then he got a switch and gave me a thrashing for it. Whenever someone spoke out of turn or misbehaved in class, the punishment was being hit on your open palms with a wooden ruler.

Upon finishing grammar school, the children usually stayed at home with their parents and helped them with the farming chores. There weren't any middle or high schools in the small villages. They were only in the large towns and the nearby cities.

Scary Stories

In the evenings, since we didn't have any electricity, or a radio to listen to, and no story books to read, it would be time for storytelling. We all gathered together at the kitchen table and listened to our mother as she told us scary stories. She had been told the same stories by her mother when she was a child. She only left one oil lamp lit in the room while telling the stories, which made them even more frightening, to the point that you would be afraid to go to sleep that night.

One story, which she told was about a man walking on an errand, along a path on a cloudy day. After walking for a while, he came to a fork in the road, where there stood a religious shrine bearing a cross. He decided to stop there and rest for a while. Later as he started walking again, he saw the sun come out, and it became very spring-like. There wasn't any more snow, and the further he walked, the warmer it seemed. Trees blossomed, and the grass grew very green. He continued walking, but the longer he walked the warmer he became, so he discarded some of his clothes. He became very tired, and he decided to take a nap under a tree. The next morning, the man was discovered lying frozen to death with hardly any clothes on. People claimed that the reason it happened was because a man had hanged himself on the cross at the shrine, and the place became cursed.

Another story, she told was about a traveling merchant, who sold all sorts of goods to the people in the various villages, which he visited. A family once bought a closed jar from the merchant, which contained some sort of decoration inside it. They put the jar on a shelf near the stove in their home. That evening as the man was sleeping next to the stove, he was suddenly pushed to the floor. Thinking that he just rolled out of his bed, he started to swear, when he heard someone swearing back at him! From then on, all kinds of peculiar things started happening in their home. Strange voices and noises were heard, and objects were constantly moving and falling especially during the night. Everyone in the family was frightened. They were convinced that an evil spirit was in the closed jar. Therefore, they decided to put it in the barn, but the odd occurrences kept on happening. The merchant eventually came back, and the homeowner returned the jar to him. Finally, everything went back to normal. It seemed that in most of the stories told, there were always evil spirits, who would try to scare or harm people, and that's what you feared most growing up.

One of the things, our mother tried to teach us was to never be cruel. She told us stories of what would happen if we were. One particular story, she told to us was about two boys who would catch birds and gouge their eyes out. When they became adults, and were married, and had children, their babies were born blind. I know now that the story was not true. When you are a child, though, you tend to believe your mother, and the story certainly got the message across.

Sibling Characteristics

Ronnie, Mary, and I were fair-skinned, with blond hair, and blue eyes. John, Tony, and Rose had brown hair, grey-brown eyes, and darker complexions. All of us were tall except Rose, who was average in height.

John and Tony were very different from each other. John was obedient, conservative, level-headed, and responsible. Tony was always more of a rebel, free-spirited, quick-tempered, and somewhat thick-headed. Ronnie was very strong-willed, responsible, and level-headed. Rose was a little passive, sensitive, and affectionate. Mary was easy going and happy. My temperament, overall, was more like that of my brother, John.

My mother said Tony was a very sweet child up until the age of two. At that time, she cut off his long hair, and after that there was a complete change in his behavior. She said it was like the Devil had gotten into him. From then on he was very disobedient, and as he grew older, he was continually getting into trouble. He was always getting into fights with the other boys in the village, and many times John would have to intercede and rescue him. As he grew up, he would constantly pick on my sisters.

Discipline

While growing up, we got along very well, always looking after one another and helping our mother with anything, she asked us to do. We never questioned, spoke out of turn, argued, or talked back to our mother as you just didn't do things like that in those days. Children were taught to abide by a strict code of behavior. You respected your elders and honored your parents.

Of course, there were times when, we were unruly just like most kids. Anytime, a child spoke out of turn or misbehaved they were corrected by the nearest older child or adult, and their parents accepted it without any objection. I don't remember our mother ever hitting any of us. When we did misbehave she would threaten us with a thrashing, but by the time she found something to hit us with, her anger would be gone. At that point, all she gave us was a good scolding.

From time to time, some of my mother's family would come by and visit us. They couldn't really do anything to help us with our situation as they, too, were very poor. I don't remember any of my grandparents. My mother's father died at a fairly young age, but my mother's mother came to visit us once in a while.

Ronnie does remember one particular time when our grandmother came to visit us. I was about six months old, and I was bundled up like a papoose asleep in a carriage. My three sisters, Ronnie, Rose, and Mary were pushing me up a hill. They decided to let the carriage roll down the hill all by itself and see what would happen. As the carriage was rolling down the hill, it hit a bump, overturned, and I tumbled out. Luckily, I was unhurt. Our grandmother witnessed the whole event and after seeing that I wasn't hurt, she gave Ronnie a good spanking and scolding as she was the oldest, and she should have known better than to do that.

My brother, John, having been raised in Zdiar in his early years did know more of my grandparents. He said that he didn't like going to visit our father's mother as whenever he did, she made him sit with her and recite 'The Holy Rosary.' She was extremely religious like our mother.

My brother, Tony, was always very inquisitive and there were times when it got him into trouble. One day, while he was nosing around at a neighbor's farm, he saw some machinery that was running. He went over to one of the machines, and somehow his forefinger got stuck in some of the gears, which severed the tip of his finger. He immediately ran home in a lot of pain, and our mother attended to him. Once my sisters and I found out what had happened, we searched the area, found his severed fingertip, and put it in a matchbox. Later in the day, we had a burial ceremony in the village cemetery. We also did that if we found a dead bird. I guess, we were just playing at being grown-ups.

Religious Holidays

The religious holidays were a very exciting and special time for us. We always looked forward to them as the Catholic Church was an important part of our lives. On religious holidays, numerous groups of people would pass through our village on pilgrimages to the Church of the Annunciation of the Blessed Virgin Mary. It was located in a city called Levoca, on the top of a steep hill, overlooking miles of the countryside. We sat on the side of the road with cups, and buckets of water, and offered it to the people as they were passing by. Usually, they gave us a small amount of money, or cookies and candy, and offered their thanks.

On Holy Saturday, the day before Easter Sunday, the women of the household gathered up all of the kielbasa, blood sausage, bacon, ham, and pork, which they were going to serve on Easter Sunday. They put it in a basket and carried it to the church, whereupon the priest would bless it. After returning from church, we were allowed to have a little snack of the blessed food. Then on Easter Sunday, everyone enjoyed the complete dinner in the early afternoon. The remaining crumbs from dinner were saved because they were considered special blessed crumbs. My mother would mix half of the crumbs with the seeds, which when planted were supposed to help the crops grow larger and better. The other half of the crumbs were mixed with the chicken feed. The belief being, that the mixture when fed to the chickens would enable them to lay more eggs.

On Easter Sunday morning, before going to church, we put coins in a wash basin, poured water into it, and then washed our hands and face with the water. Supposedly, that meant you would prosper financially during the coming year. Then on Easter Monday, the boys in the village cut off a branch from a willow tree, and gently hit all the girls with it, and then doused them with water. Apparently, that ensured all of the girls would be healthy during the course of the year.

December 5th, the Eve of St. Mikulas Day (St. Nicholas Day) was a special day for children. All of us cleaned our shoes, and each of us placed one of our shoes on the window sill of the living room. Later that night, when we were all in bed and fast asleep, our mother would come into our bedroom holding a candle and awaken all of us. Sleepy-eyed, we saw her standing there in the dimly lit room with St. Mikulas. He had a long white beard, and he wore a full length white gown with a red cape over it. Upon his head was a red bishop's hat, and he carried a curved golden staff.

Lurking behind St. Mikulas was the Devil. He was dressed in a long black gown with a red hooded cape. He was intimidating to look at, with his face painted all black, horns on the top of his head, and wearing a heavy metal chain around his waist. The Devil would frighten us by making all kinds of strange faces and noises. He was very scary! It was then that St. Mikulas, asked all of us if we had been good or bad during the year. Of course, no one would ever admit that they had been bad. The next morning, upon awakening, all of us ran into the living room to find our shoes on the window sill. Each of us, who had been good, found our shoe filled with various cookies and candies. Anyone, who had misbehaved found in their shoe a rotten apple wrapped in a soiled piece of paper, and underneath they found only a few cookies and candies.

Every December 13th, which was the day after, St. Lucy Day, each family in the village contributed flour to the priest in the church. The priest would have all of the flour mixed with other ingredients and made into round wafers, which were then baked. Then he blessed all of the wafers before having them distributed to every family in the village. These wafers were called 'Oplatky.' Oplatky was a Communion-like wafer with a scene of the Nativity imprinted upon it. It was an important part of the Christmas Eve celebration.

On Christmas Eve, we decorated our Christmas tree, which we had chopped down from the nearby woods a day or two earlier. While we were decorating, our mother would be baking all kinds of cakes and cookies, filling the house with the wonderful aroma of the baked goods. My mother also prepared the dinner table by putting some hay under the tablecloth to symbolize Jesus' humble birth in the manger. All of us children were outside looking for the first star of the evening, as dinner could not start until the star was in sight. Prior to dinner, we said our prayers followed by the breaking and eating of the oplatky, which our mother had spread with honey.

A traditional meatless dinner started with a soup made with noodles in a plum broth, as it was a Slovak custom in our area. The soup was followed by buchti, a very light dumpling covered with melted butter. The rest of the meal usually consisted of pierogies, which were stuffed with potato and cheese or other various fillings. We also had fish, potatoes, and sauerkraut. Once we had finished with the main meal, we enjoyed some of the delicious cakes and cookies, which our mother had baked. Then she read us the story of the birth of Jesus from the Bible. Afterwards, we all sang Slovak Christmas carols. Later, my sisters and some of their friends went out caroling in the village. Usually, the people showed their appreciation by giving them cookies or candy.

Then we went to Midnight Mass in the nearby village of Velbahi. A procession was formed by our neighbors and we joined in. Everyone walked in the snow, singing Christmas carols, along the way with lanterns aglow. It was very cold, and the snow was glistening. There were some woods and valleys, which we had to walk through before we reached the village and the church. We dressed warmly in the winter, but our feet were always cold as we didn't have the best of shoes or socks, to be able to walk with in the snow. Therefore, we tried to walk as quickly as we could. When we returned home, we put our wet shoes and socks by the warm stove to dry them.

To celebrate the birth of Jesus in the manger, all of us children went into the barn. We climbed up to the hay loft to sleep while the few animals, we still had slept in their stalls below. We spent the whole night sleeping there until the next morning.

A priest from the church usually visited our home in the early morning on Christmas Day. He blessed our house and looked for offerings. We presented him with either money or some food.

On Christmas Day, my mother burned the same incense, which was used in the church that she had received from the priest. She heated it in a pan until it started to smoke. Then it filled the whole room with its unique scent. If you shut your eyes, you felt as if you were in church.

Prior to Christmas dinner, we started by saying our daily prayers as we always did before we had any dinner. The main course served was usually either baked ham or roast pork with all the trimmings. For dessert we had the various cakes, which our mother had baked made with poppy seeds, prune jam, crushed walnuts, and cinnamon. She also made large sugar cookies and sprinkled them with cinnamon. They were cut into small pieces before serving.

No one ever received any Christmas presents as there was never any money for them. However, we did have our Christmas tree, which was decorated beautifully with lots of goodies on it. Our tree was adorned with white candles, and a red paper chain, which was wrapped around the tree. There were homemade gingerbread cookies shaped like stars and other various shapes. Some of them were decorated with sugar frosting and tiny bits of candy. Other cookies had on them a paper picture with images such as: the baby Jesus, an angel, the Nativity, or a scenic picture of a church or animals.

In addition, there were hard candies wrapped in colorful papers and shiny red apples. On the top of the tree there was a lovely glass angel. During the day, our mother would hoist the Christmas tree up to the ceiling with a rope, where it stayed suspended until she decided to lower it again. The reason being, that we might be tempted to pick off some of the cookies and sweets from it when she was not there. We were never allowed to lower the tree unless we had her approval.

Once the twelve days of Christmas were over, and all the apples, cookies, and candies were gone from the tree, all of us children took it outdoors. We stuck it in the ground, and then we decorated it again with the empty candy wrappers and all sorts of other things that we found. Then we just stood there and admired it.

The Difficult Times

After working in the factory in Hastings for a few years and rooming in a boarding house, my father met an elderly widow. In time, they developed a close relationship, and she allowed him to board at her two-family home, rent-free. He looked after her and helped with the various chores, which needed to be done. However, even living rent-free my father still sent very little money to my mother. She constantly, wrote and pleaded with him to send her money. When he finally did send some, usually, it was only a single dollar in the envelope, which didn't do very much to help our situation.

My father had been in America for a few years, when he realized that it would be impossible for him to earn enough money to return to Czechoslovakia and repay his debts. He wrote to my mother and said that he decided to remain in America, but somehow he would find a way to send for us. We hoped and prayed that soon, we would be able to join him there.

With little or no money coming from our father in America, our situation was becoming desperate. Our mother was forced to sell some of the farm animals as she could not afford to feed them, and the money was needed to purchase items for the household. As time passed, it got to the point where we were left with only one cow and some chickens, which our mother didn't sell as they were needed for milk and eggs. Unfortunately, the bank confiscated the fields that we planted crops on, to pay down some of the debt owed to them, leaving us with only our garden.

I remember one particular day when my mother and Uncle Gustin bought a pig from a neighbor. With the help of the neighbors, they proceeded to slaughter the pig. I was there as they killed it, but ran away after a very short time as the poor pig was squealing very loudly. I felt terrible listening to it suffering with pain. Afterward, I decided to never witness anything like that ever again! For a time, the slaughtered pig provided us with meat, which we cured in the smokehouse. Besides the different cuts of meat, we made bacon, and various sausages. We let no part of the carcass go to waste.

In the summertime, we always had fresh fruit and vegetables from the garden. During the winter months, things were always more difficult as we had to rely on the foods, which we had stored in the root cellar. Eventually, we would exhaust that supply, and we had to do without or rely on our neighbors for help.

There were many times, when we just ate a piece of flat bread with a little butter on it with tea, or a slice of bread with chicken fat and sliced onion for breakfast. I remember times when we no longer had any more potatoes left to eat. Thankfully, the local farmers allowed us to go into their fields and gather up all the leftover potatoes, which hadn't been picked.

To make tea, my mother picked the blossoms from the linden tree, which was near our house, and then dried them in the sun, and put them in a container. The dried leaves made a flavorful cup of tea. There was a grass called 'Schav' that grew in a certain open field near our home. It was a luscious leafy grass, which had a tangy sweet-sour-salty taste. It did help when our stomachs were hungry and growling. After eating it, our teeth, tongue, and gums were a bright shade of green. Other times we went into the garden, pulled out a carrot, rinsed it in the nearby brook, and ate it. Sometimes when there weren't any more cucumbers left in our garden, I crawled into our neighbor's cucumber patch underneath the large leaves and vines, while on my hands and knees (so I wouldn't be seen) and sampled a few of his cucumbers. Of course, I didn't dare tell my mother because I knew, if I did, I would get a good scolding.

To ease the burden of feeding us, our mother sent my two brothers, John at fourteen, and Tony at twelve years old to work on other farms in the area. While there, they earned their keep and a little bit of money. They came home only on the weekends. One time my brother, John, went to work for a farmer, who forced him to sleep in the barn with the animals. He didn't voice any objection because he was afraid that the farmer would dismiss him, and our mother desperately needed the money, which he earned. John also wasn't fed by the farmer like he should have been. Upon returning home at the end of the week, he was very hungry and was covered with lice from head to foot. Our mother had to boil all the clothes he wore and pretty much had to delouse his entire body as well. Of course, John never returned to work on that farm.

When John was fifteen years of age, Uncle Gustin was able to find him a job as an apprentice at a ski and bike shop in the city of Poprad. He slept in the back room of the shop, and his meals were provided by his employer. On the weekends, he borrowed a bicycle from the shop and come home. It was a long trip, twenty-eight miles from Trstany, several hours each way. Once home he gave our mother the money, which he had earned during the prior week. My brother, Tony, stayed at home helping our mother with the household chores as Uncle Gustin had married and moved to Hincovce, a little village, a short distance from us. John, the oldest of us children became the man of the house, and we all depended on him.

Often, my mother would go to work in the fields for other farmers to earn some money as well. She gathered up crops, tied up bales of hay, and tended to livestock. I remember that she always worked very hard. Ronnie, being the oldest of my sisters was given the responsibility of caring for me, Mary, and Rose. When our mother was gone, she was in charge. In essence, she was like a second mother to us. As we all grew older and Ronnie finished school, she went to work caring for some young children in our village while their parents tended to their farm. Usually, Ronnie brought home some food, which the parents of the children gave her as they knew of our plight and wanted to help.

Prior to my father's departure to America our house consisted of five large rooms. Little by little, things became more and more difficult after he left. By 1937, we were in a dire situation. We lived in only one room of the house as it was easier to heat and maintain. We were also forced to sell the one cow, we still had. Whenever, our mother needed more money she sold off more and more of our furniture to be able to purchase food, which we so desperately needed. Mary and I slept in one bed that we shared with our mother.

When the bed that my sisters, Ronnie and Rose, slept on was sold, they had to sleep on a bench, which opened up into a bed with only thick blankets to serve as a mattress. John and Tony's beds were also sold. They slept on the wooden floor on top of two large burlap bags filled with straw and a goose down comforter for a blanket. Every morning, they rolled up the burlap bags and stored them away until the evening. During the cold and snowy winters, we all slept as close as possible to the stove trying to keep warm at night.

Every evening, we all gathered together around the kitchen table and kneeled down on the bare hardwood floor, using our chairs to lean on for support. We recited 'The Holy Rosary' numerous times. While our mother led with the 'Hail Mary,' we followed with the 'Holy Mary.' By the time we finished praying, our knees would be aching with pain. We did that for as long as I can remember while growing up in Czechoslovakia.

Furthermore, our mother constantly prayed throughout the day to God and the Virgin Mary for help, hoping that we soon would be able to go to America. There were many times, when things looked very grim and hopeless. However, my mother's faith in God never wavered. She knew in her heart, that sooner or later, our prayers would be answered.

My Mother's Dedication

While I was growing up, I never fully realized all of the difficulties and hardships, which my mother went through and had to endure. It seems at that time, we all took things for granted, and we didn't think to give her the credit, which she, so rightfully deserved. Looking back now, I truly appreciate how fortunate, we were to have had a mother, who sacrificed everything for her children. My mother was blessed with a very loving, caring, and unselfish heart. She was wise well beyond her years, and she must have had a tremendously strong constitution to be able to accomplish all that she did.

Her first thought was always her children and our well-being. Even though, she only had a grammar school education, she had a great sense of values, which she tried to teach to all of us, along with a lot of pure common sense. My mother was very honest and deeply compassionate. We were all very devoted to her and tried to follow the example, she had set for us. She was just a wonderful person and was liked by everyone, who knew her.

As far as I am concerned, she is the closest person to a saint, I ever knew. I can't imagine what life must have been like for her trying to support six children, working in the fields, and not having a husband to help her. She wasn't physically affectionate toward us, mostly because she really didn't have the time to be so. We never really required it to be reassured of her love as we were all very secure. All we had to do was be in her presence, and look into her eyes, and in our hearts we would feel the tremendous amount of love and caring that she possessed for each of us. We were truly blessed in having been given such a wonderful mother!

Chapter 3:

THE JOURNEY TO AMERICA

The Threat of War

When my father first left for America in 1930, my mother thought, he would return to us within a few years, but that was not to be. Before long it was the year 1937, and Hitler was in power and had complete control of Germany. He had annexed Austria and next was setting his sights on the Sudetenland. Three million citizens of Czechoslovakia, the Sudeten Germans, lived in the northern, western, and southern border regions (the Sudetenland) of the new state, which was formed after the collapse of the Hapsburg Monarchy in 1918. In the 1930's, Hitler's Germany demanded that these regions be incorporated into the Third Reich. The Sudetenland was a rich and prosperous portion of Czechoslovakia. It possessed vast industrial and agricultural areas, which Hitler needed for his conquest of Europe.

Therefore, with the threat of aggression and a possible war with Germany, looming on the horizon, Czechoslovakia instituted the draft and began mobilizing its Armed Forces. I remember the Army staging military maneuvers near our village. I was surprised and thrilled when I found a brass whistle in the grass, which one of the soldiers must have lost. That brass whistle was a cherished treasure to me. I played with it for the longest time as it was the only toy, I ever had.

There was now the possibility of my eldest brother, John, being drafted into the Armed Forces as soon, he would be eighteen years old. Our mother feared that might happen, so she constantly wrote to our father begging him to send money for John's passage to America. A local superstition was spreading throughout the community because of the unusual red sky, which appeared daily for a number of days. It foretold of a terrible war, the red signifying all of the blood that was going to be shed. The elderly people claimed that they saw the same red sky before the First World War, which resulted in millions of people losing their lives.

John Arrives in America and Safety

Thankfully, the money for John's passage arrived! Soon, he was on his way to America and safety, aboard the R.M.S. Aquitania. Upon reaching New York City, John resided with our father in Hastings for a short time. Then he moved out on his own as he didn't approve of our father's lifestyle. Fortunately, John befriended a Slovak family, who lived in the city. They took a great liking to him, inviting him to live in their home, and treated him as if he were a member of their family. They helped him with the new language, and they also found him employment at the Hotel New Yorker in Manhattan doing janitorial duties. Eventually, he was transferred into the kitchen as a kitchen helper, where he was able to eat his meals for free. From time-to-time, my father asked John for money. He said he had borrowed the money, in order to bring John to America, so it needed to be repaid. John also sent our mother money, whenever he could, as he knew that she desperately needed it.

John attended night school for a time, but it was only briefly as he was constantly working. He was pretty much self-taught. I tried to imagine how difficult and scary everything must have been for him. There he was just seventeen years of age, mostly on his own in a foreign country, where he didn't even speak the language.

Our Prayers are Answered

In the meantime, things were going from bad to worse in Europe. Everyone was now worried about Germany's territorial aspirations and military threats. Our mother was still constantly writing to our father, pleading with him, to please help us come to America. She was extremely anxious, as things at home were becoming more and more difficult and frightening.

In the early summer of 1938, the widow, who my father was a companion to became very ill and was diagnosed with terminal cancer. Realizing that she had just a short time to live, she decided to provide the funds for our passage to America. It was her dying wish to see us reunited with our father. Our constant prayers were not in vain. God and the Virgin Mary, had indeed, heard our prayers for all those years, and they were answered by having the widow come to our aid.

In order for us to be admitted to the United States, our father was required to fill out an Affidavit of Support to prove his family would not become a burden to the State. He falsified the affidavit claiming, he owned a four-family house, worth twelve thousand, five hundred dollars. He also wrote, stating that he was employed as a bartender with a steady income. In truth, he worked in a factory, earning a modest salary and didn't own any property. It was fortunate for us that the agency never chose to investigate his claims because if they had, I'm not sure if we would have been allowed to enter the United States.

Preparing to Leave Home

As soon as our father learned, we would be allowed to enter the United States, he sent word to our mother that with the help of the widow, we would finally be able to leave Czechoslovakia and join him in America. Our mother was overjoyed, thanking God and the Virgin Mary for answering our prayers. Then she immediately began making preparations for our journey. We were all thrilled and excited, that at last, we were to be on our way. I remember telling all my playmates the news. There we were, only knowing the world of our small rural village, which we grew up in, preparing to experience life in a much different part of the world.

Like everyone, we thought everybody in America was rich, and that it was the land of milk and honey. Occasionally, we received post cards from our father showing pictures of the New York City skyline. It looked very clean and majestic. We thought, by coming to America that our days of being poor and hungry were over. We believed that our mother was going to be happy and not have any more worries, and we were all going to have a better life with our father taking care of us.

It was necessary for everyone in the family to have a physical examination, to make sure that we were all in good health. All of us children did fine. However, our mother was found to have a large number of missing and decayed teeth. Furthermore, she was told, she needed to have all her remaining teeth extracted. Only then, would she be issued a passport to enter into the United States.

Shortly after being informed that her decayed teeth needed to be removed, our mother walked to a dentist in a nearby village. There was no one to accompany her as Tony and Gustin were both working, and Ronnie had to stay at home caring for Rose, Mary, and me, so our mother went alone to the dentist. It was late in the afternoon, while we were all waiting and watching for our mother to return home, when our sister, Ronnie, saw our mother coming over the hill. She was stooped over, walking very slowly, and stumbling. Her clothes were splattered with blood, and her face contorted with pain. Ronnie ran to her and embraced her. Both of them were crying. Our mother leaned on Ronnie for support, the rest of the way home. Upon arriving home, she immediately went to bed. We were all deeply worried about her and felt terrible seeing her lying there in pain, unable to help her. She was only able to consume broth or milk until her gums healed. It took several days, before she was well enough to be up and around. She wouldn't be getting her new dentures until after we were settled in America.

In those days, every one of us had problems with decaying teeth. Although, none of us were taught much about dental hygiene, we did use our fingers to brush our teeth with some sort of powder that our mother gave us. It was only later, while in the United States, that we were taught how to clean our teeth regularly with a toothbrush and toothpaste.

The Start of Our Journey

It was in September of 1938, when we received our passports and the paperwork for our trip to America. Soon, we would be leaving the only home that we had ever known. Prior to our departure, our mother sold the few remaining articles of any value and the furniture, which we had left. We bid farewell to our neighbors. They were all very happy to learn that after all the terrible years of struggling, we were going to be on our way to America. After loading our few meager belongings onto the horse and wagon, we started on our way to Poprad where we were to board the train and begin the long journey to France. As we left, we watched our village disappear from our view, thinking that we were never going to see it again.

The train ride was a new experience for us as we had never been on one before. We were supposed, to take the train all the way through Germany to Cherbourg, France, where we would board the ship, which was to take us across the Atlantic Ocean to America. Unfortunately, upon reaching Prague, eight tiring hours later, we were told, we could go no further. Czechoslovakia had declared martial law, and the borders were closed. The situation between Czechoslovakia and Germany was escalating. Hitler was still negotiating, with the major powers to annex the Sudetenland, and if the Allies did not give in to his demands, he was threatening to take it by military force.

We were housed in a section of a large building temporarily with a number of other people, who were also immigrating. A large number of Jewish people were there as well. They were trying to escape the terrible persecution and horrific crimes, that Hitler would ultimately inflict upon their people. Our living quarters were somewhat crowded, there was no privacy, and everyone had to sleep on cots. The constant waiting to find out when the borders would once again be opened was very stressful.

While walking through Prague, we noticed the presence of a number of soldiers and tanks. Everyone was deeply worried about the fact that Czechoslovakia might go to war with Germany. One day, while we were walking in the city, Ronnie noticed a young boy peeling an orange. She was curious because she had never seen one before, so she asked him if she could look at it. When she did, the young boy squeezed the orange, and the juice from it squirted into her eyes. The young boy ran away laughing. Unfortunately, Ronnie's introduction to oranges wasn't a pleasant one. During our stay in Prague it was also the first time, we had ever tasted ice cream. Our mother bought one dish of it, which we all shared.

After being in Prague, for about a week or so, and anxiously waiting to continue our journey, we were told that we would have to return home. The borders were still closed. No one knew for certain when they would reopen again, or what was going to happen in the days to come. The tedious negotiations in Munich, with Hitler and the Allies, were still going on. During that period of time while in Prague, we spent most of our meager funds buying food. We were forced to leave Prague with very little money. Therefore, with no other place to go, we decided to return back to our village, Trstany. However, now there was no place for us to live as our house had been confiscated by the bank once we had left. Another family was now living there. We were all very depressed, especially our mother as the future looked frighteningly uncertain.

Having had to use the remainder of our money to purchase the train tickets for our return to Trstany, we had nothing left to buy food with for the long train ride. Our mother then went into a restaurant, explained our problem, and begged the owner for some food. He took pity on us, and gave our mother a large bag of fried bacon bits, along with some bread, which sustained us until we were back home in our village.

Returning Home

Upon reaching Trstany, we were a wretched sight, as all of us were very tired and hungry with the look of desolation in our eyes. We were greeted by a number of our neighbors and our uncle, Gustin. All of them were extremely surprised to see us again. They thought that, by this time, we were well on our way to America. They were very upset and felt sorry for us, so much, that some of them were even brought to tears. There we were, back home again, but even worse off than before we had left. Now, we were homeless. Fortunately, we had very compassionate neighbors, who volunteered to take us into their homes and treated us like family. We were split up, each one of us going to live with a different family for a time. Rose, Mary, and I resumed our schooling until we were once again able to leave Czechoslovakia. After coming home from school, we helped with the chores, which needed to be done for the various families, we were living with. Ronnie continued caring for the little children, who had been in her care before we left Trstany as she now lived with that family. My mother and Tony also helped with the daily duties needing to be done for the neighbors, whom they were living with.

As soon as she was able to, our mother wrote to our father and John, informing them of our dire predicament. In earnest, she asked them to send us money as soon as they could, so that we would be able to survive until we could resume our journey. The mail in those days was very slow. A letter usually took twelve or fourteen days to reach America. The wait for a return letter was very trying.

After living with our neighbors for about two months, our mother felt that we had imposed on them long enough. She was also very unhappy, due to the fact that we were all living separately. She pleaded with the bank to let us use a vacant house, which they possessed in our village. Fortunately, the bank allowed us to live in the house for as long as was necessary. All of us were very happy to be living together again. The house, though, was empty of any and all furnishings except for the wood burning stove. Our neighbors, once again were very kind. They lent us a kitchen table with some chairs and benches, some cookware, and other essentials, which we needed. With some money coming from America, along with help from our neighbors and our uncle, Gustin, we were able to manage for the duration.

As we had no beds to sleep on, we were forced to sleep on the cold hardwood floor, using burlap bags filled with straw for our beds. Our mother, at least, still had the goose down comforters to cover us up with. We all slept next to each other and as close to the stove as possible, trying to stay warm during those cold winter nights. We had no money to be able to purchase firewood for cooking or heating. Therefore, we went into the nearby woods almost every day, with our mother to gather some firewood, walking through the cold deep snow. Each of us carried a burlap sack to put the fallen scraps of twigs and branches into, which we found on the forest floor.

We eagerly awaited some news, which would enable us to once again continue on our way. We still didn't have any electricity, and no one in the village owned any radios. You had to go to the nearest city and buy a newspaper, in order to learn about the latest events. All of us were terribly worried that if a war should break out with Germany, we would never be able to leave Czechoslovakia, and then what would become of us.

We continued to say our prayers, every evening, praying that the Sudetenland crisis would soon be resolved, so that we would be able to leave for America. Our last Christmas in Trstany was not a very joyous one. We didn't have a Christmas tree. There was no traditional Christmas Eve dinner and none of the delicious cakes and cookies, which our mother used to bake. However, we did attend Midnight Mass, and we had a simple dinner on Christmas Day.

The Final Journey

Then in January of 1939, thankfully, the borders were once again opened! The Allies had given in to Hitler's demands to take possession of the Sudetenland. What the Allies hadn't realized, at that time, was by appeasing Hitler it would only lead to World War II. They sacrificed a large portion of Czechoslovakia for what they thought would satisfy Hitler's territorial claims. We were pleased to hear the news that the negotiations were resolved. Therefore, we could now, finally continue our journey to America, but we were also upset that a large part of our country was gone.

Our mother started planning to leave immediately. She wrote to our father, and pleaded with him to send us some additional money to help us pay for the train tickets and other things, which we needed for the trip. Much to our chagrin, he wrote back claiming that he was unable to send us the funds, which we so urgently needed. You cannot imagine how shocked and deeply saddened, we all were to learn that. Our mother then wrote to John, telling him what had transpired. Once John read the letter, telling him of our desperate circumstances, he went to his employer and begged him for an advance of his salary. When his employer was told of the reason why John needed the money, he sympathetically advanced it to him. We were overjoyed and greatly relieved when the money finally came!

In early February of 1939, we once again packed our few belongings and loaded them onto the horse and wagon. Soon, we would be on our way to Poprad to board the train, for the long and exhausting ride, which we had taken several months earlier. We thanked our neighbors, for the tremendous amount of help that they had given us. We were again on our way to France to board the ship, which was going to take us to America. We prayed the whole way, that this time, we wouldn't be turned back, and that we would be able to complete our journey.

When we reached the German border, the armed and intimidating Nazi police with their Nazi armbands and austere look on their faces, boarded the train to inspect our passports. Everyone was afraid and very nervous thinking they might arrest us, and then we would be trapped there with no one to help us. Thankfully, we were able to continue on the rest of the way without any incidents. Traveling through the German countryside, we noticed the Nazi Swastika and military personnel everywhere, which also contributed to our extreme anxiety. When we finally reached the border of France and safety, we breathed a big sigh of relief. After many more long hours on the train, which seemed like an eternity to me, we reached the harbor in Cherbourg, France.

Boarding Our Ship

Our ship was the R.M.S. Aquitania, the same ship, which brought John to America. It was named 'The Ship Beautiful' because of its luxurious accommodations. Of course, only the more affluent passengers could afford the luxury cabins and the ship's amenities that it offered.

It was the first time, that any of us had seen an actual ship. The ship was very intimidating as we looked up at it with its four huge smokestacks spewing out white smoke and its tremendous size. It was also the first time, that we had ever seen the ocean. We were all very excited to finally be on our way. Traveling on a ship was to be a new experience for us and one that we were all looking forward to, but as it turned out, it wasn't anything like we imagined it would be.

Upon boarding, we were assigned to our tiny cabins at the very bottom and rear section of the ship. All three cabins were situated next to each other, and there were two to a cabin, Tony and I in one, Rose and Mary in another, and our mother and Ronnie in the third one. I don't know if there was a fourth-class section on the ship, but if there was, that's where we were. It's very possible, the widow gave our father ample funds to purchase better accommodations for us on the ship, but in turn, he may have purchased the cheapest ones, thus deciding to keep the rest of the funds for himself. I think he was born with larceny in his heart.

S. S. Aquitania, Cunard Line,
New York, Cherbourg, Southampton

The Long Voyage

During the entire voyage, we had to endure the fumes and the continuous rumbling noise from the engine and the ship's propellers, along with the rough seas, which were typical for February. It was very difficult to sleep. After being on the ship for a while, we encountered a very bad winter storm. It was extremely windy, the waves were tremendously high, the ship was being buffered from side to side, and rolling up and down. By then, almost everyone in the family was seasick, to the point, they couldn't eat anything. My sister, Mary, and I were the only ones, who didn't get sick.

After a few days, once the storm at sea had subsided and everyone was feeling better, they were able to eat regular food, except our mother. She became so dehydrated from being sick that she actually threw up blood. We were all deeply concerned about her health. The only nourishment, she could take was in the form of liquids. Eventually, we were told by the ship's stewards that we should take her to the ship's clinic, where they were able to give her some medicine for motion sickness. We all thanked God, when a few days later, our mother started to feel better and was able to eat solid food.

One day when the seas were finally calm, and everyone was feeling better, my mother and sisters decided to go up on deck. They enjoyed breathing in the fresh sea air, after being cooped up in the cabins for so long. After spending some time on deck in the sun and ocean wind, they returned to their cabins. Later that day, they all suffered from a serious case of windburn.

The porters came into our cabins almost every morning to sanitize the floors because of the constant humidity, which caused mold and mildew, along with germs. They used a cleaning product with a terrible odor that made everyone somewhat nauseous.

Mary and I frequently explored the ship as it was difficult staying in the cabins all the time. However, we were limited by the ship's crew as to, which areas of the ship we were allowed to go on.

I don't recall, what kind of food we were served, but I do remember eating a banana for the first time, and to me, it was tasteless. While growing up in Czechoslovakia, I had been accustomed to eating the sweet fresh fruit, which we picked from the fruit trees on our farm.

The journey seemed endless. We began to wonder, if we were ever going to reach the shores of America. All we could see was water, water, everywhere. We never imagined, there could be, so much water in the world!

Chapter 4:

OUR NEW BEGINNING IN AMERICA

Our Ship Arrives in America

It was seven long arduous days, into our voyage when on the morning of February 17th, 1939, we finally reached the shores of America. After having breakfast and returning to our cabins, we heard a lot of commotion and excitement in the corridors of the ship. Curious as to what was going on, we soon learned that our ship was nearing the New York City harbor. We rushed to join the hundreds of other immigrants, on the cold and windy deck of the ship, to view the New York City skyline. Although, we don't recall seeing the Statue of Liberty we probably did, but we didn't realize the significance of it. We were, however, completely awed by the New York City skyscrapers, which were so numerous and looked so magnificent gleaming against the bright clear sky. All of us were very happy that, at last, we were going to set our feet upon dry land. We then returned to our cabins and began making preparations to leave the ship.

Meeting My Father

We docked at the New York City Pier. After searching the enormous crowd of people, we saw our father and our brother, John, waiting for us, down below on the dock. It was a strange moment for me, as it was the first time that I had ever seen my father. I wasn't sure what to expect as the only parent, I had ever known was my loving mother. My mother was ill at ease, even apprehensive, about seeing her husband again. Having lived apart from him, for so long, he was a virtual stranger to her.

Arriving at Our New Home

After we had disembarked and while we were going through customs, we noticed people of all different nationalities and manner of dress, which seemed strange to us. Moreover, we must have appeared the same way to them. After meeting up with John and our father, we were driven to our new home in the town of Hastings-on-the-Hudson, New York. It was about fifteen miles, north of Manhattan. Our father still lived in the same two-family house, which belonged to the widow. She was living on the first floor of the house, and we would be living on the second floor.

Our Angel in America

Once we arrived at the house, we spent a few minutes dropping off our luggage in our apartment on the second floor. Then our first priority was to go downstairs to see the widow. We felt such a deep sense of gratitude to her. Although, very ill and bedridden, she was very eager and happy to be able to finally meet all of us. Upon meeting her, our mother hugged, kissed, and thanked her for the wonderful gift, she had bestowed on all of us, by paying for our passage to America. Then each of us took turns, hugging, kissing, and expressing our thanks to her as well. We visited her daily. My sisters would sing various religious Slovak songs to her, which she enjoyed listening to very much.

After a few weeks, the widow was transferred to the hospital as her health was rapidly deteriorating. We continued to visit her there for the next several days, until she passed away. She was a very special and loving person, to have been able, to do what she did for us without ever having met us. It seems, she just wasn't ready to go, until she knew that we were all safely in America. To this day, I don't know of anyone else, who would be so compassionate and generous. It was unfortunate, that there was not enough time for us to really get to know her.

It took us almost nine years, to follow our father to America, and it was only because of her that we were able to do so. She truly was our salvation. I can't imagine, what our life would have been like, if we had never left Czechoslovakia. All of our lives were changed, by her one act of overwhelming generosity, love, and deep compassion. I think if, we had to depend on our father to bring us to America, we probably, would have remained in Czechoslovakia.

Our Bitter Disappointment

The house was situated at the bottom of a steep hill, next to some freight yards, on the banks of the Hudson River. Our apartment on the second floor of the house was very small. It had a kitchen, living room, three bedrooms, a bathroom with a flush toilet, and hot-cold running water. Having these conveniences was very new to us. My parents slept in one bedroom, my three sisters in another, and Tony and me in the third one.

The freight yards next to our house were a source of constant noise, with countless freight cars going by daily and blasting their whistles, while their engines were spewing enormous amounts of smoke and black soot into the air. There were also a large number of factories with huge smokestacks billowing white smoke, contributing to the unhealthy air, which lingered in the area for some time. We were often startled by the loud whistles, which the various factories sounded off several times a day. It took a while, before we became accustomed to all the noise.

We were in disbelief, as it was not at all what we expected or envisioned. In Czechoslovakia, people spoke of America as if it was some sort of a paradise. Therefore, you can imagine our bitter disappointment, when we arrived here and found, that it was not at all like they described. It was a far cry from our home in Czechoslovakia, where we had fruit trees and woods surrounding our village. We also had beautiful pastures of grass, and fields of vegetable crops, and the constant fresh air, which blew in from the nearby mountains.

Here we were, coming from a quiet little corner of the world, to the hustle and bustle of a large town with autos, buses, and trains. It was very different now having concrete sidewalks, black-top roads, continuous noise, and crowds of people everywhere. While living in our village, we knew everyone. We were now in a strange new land where we didn't know anyone except our father, and we didn't know the language. Nevertheless, we were thankful to be in America. We had no choice, but to try and make the best of it.

Adjusting to Our New Life

About a month after we arrived in America, our father had a little homecoming party for us at a local restaurant to celebrate our arrival. After a while, I went outside, and there were some boys there, who were talking, pointing, and laughing at me. I guess that, it was because I was poorly dressed and still wearing Slovakian clothes. I was also still pretty bald as my mother had cut off all my hair, before we left Czechoslovakia. Although, I didn't understand any English, it was obvious to me that I was being made fun of. I decided, I wasn't going to stand for it, so I started fighting with them, and then they ran off. In the meantime, someone went and informed my father that I was outside fighting with some boys.

I remember that I was sitting on a fence when my father came out. He was very angry and never even asked me why I was fighting. Instead, he yelled at me, grabbed me by the ear, and yanked me off the fence, which really hurt me quite a bit. Then he gave me a smack on my butt and brought me back inside the restaurant. It wasn't an ideal way to start a relationship with a son, whom you only recently met for the first time. I swear to this day, because of that, the one ear is longer than the other. Needless to say, I realized then, we weren't going to be the best of friends.

When we arrived in America, Tony was fifteen years old, Ronnie was thirteen, Rose was eleven, Mary was nine, and I was seven. As we were all fairly young, it was easier for us to make the adjustment from a small farming village to a large populous town. Our mother, though, had a more difficult time of it. Living in Hastings-on-the-Hudson was a lot different from our home in Europe. Here, there were stores with windows displaying all kinds of products. I remember one particular day when I was window shopping. There was a toy store, which had a beautiful silver cap pistol displayed in the store window, and 'oh' how I would have loved to have it, but of course, it was just a dream. We never received any spending money from our father to buy toys, candy, ice cream, or other goodies.

Our father accompanied our mother to the various stores when she needed to buy groceries, as she didn't yet know how to speak English. He would buy day-old Danish pastry, which we would have for our breakfast, along with coffee. Although, it wasn't very nutritious it was filling. Usually, for dinner our mother cooked low budget, traditional Slovak meals. It was very difficult for us to live on our father's salary as there were seven of us and the money, he earned didn't go very far.

My father spent most of his evenings and weekends in a bar. As young as I was, I thought that he worked there. One day, Ronnie informed me that he worked in a factory. It was only then, that I realized the reason, why he spent so much of his time in a bar was because he was drinking.

Sometimes my sisters and I walked along the railroad tracks, which were right by our home. Our sister, Ronnie, often found some money amongst the railroad ties. She was always very lucky, that way. Then we went to the local candy store and bought what we could with the money that she found.

We were soon enrolled in the public school system in Hastings. We were learning for the first time, how to read, write, and speak English. We were always the oldest and tallest in our various classes. At that time, the only clothes we had were the ones, which we brought with us from Czechoslovakia. Our father would receive old clothes from people he knew, who had children. Our mother altered them, by hand, as best she could. However, they were still old clothes, and they never fit properly. We were deeply embarrassed and ashamed having to wear them. Our classmates constantly teased and laughed at us. We must have appeared pretty strange to everyone, the four of us holding hands while marching up the street on our way to school, my three sisters with their long braids hanging down below their shoulders, and there I was with hardly any hair on my head.

Whenever, we did get different clothes to wear, they were always bought from a second-hand store. For the longest time, I remember wearing shoes, which were always too tight. Eventually, I developed hammertoes from wearing tight shoes. In those days, if you wore out the soles of your shoes you would put pieces of either cardboard or newspaper in them, so you could wear them much longer. Of course, if it rained, your feet became soaking wet. We always banded together whenever we went out, never venturing too far from home because we weren't familiar with the area, and we didn't want to get lost. It was almost impossible for us to make friends as we hadn't yet learned to speak English. Fortunately, we always had each other.

A few weeks after we arrived, our father was able to find Tony a job as a dishwasher at a local restaurant. Luckily, he didn't have to know the language to be able to wash dishes. After working all day, he attended night school trying to learn how to read and write English. At times, our father would take Tony's salary from his employer, and Tony wouldn't see any of it. He claimed that Tony owed him that money for bringing him to America. Our brother, John, continued to live with the Slovak family, who took him in, and he still worked at the Hotel New Yorker. John visited our mother and gave her some money, whenever he could afford to do so.

Germany Invades Czechoslovakia

After being in America for about a month, we heard the tragic news on the morning of March 15th, 1939. Devastated, the people of Prague woke up to see German troops marching into their city. Czechoslovakia no longer existed as a free nation, as they were now occupied by a foreign power. The borders were once again closed. We realized then how extremely fortunate, we were in being able to leave Czechoslovakia when we did.

Life with Our Father

Our father continued his drinking ways, which caused a lot of discord in the family. He was very irresponsible. After living the single life for almost nine years, he found it very difficult to cope with the responsibility of taking care of a wife and five children. His life style had completely changed, and apparently it was not to his liking. We felt, he never loved us as he never showed us any care or affection. I don't think that any of us ever viewed him as our father. We soon realized, we couldn't count on him or trust him with our welfare.

We had been living in America for just a few months, and we still weren't too familiar with the language or the neighborhood when our father disappeared for a number of days. We had no idea what had happened to him. Our mother was afraid, that perhaps, he decided to leave us again. What would we do if he had? How would we live? What our mother feared the most was, what if the authorities learned that we were now living alone with no means of support. Would they send us back to Czechoslovakia? While waiting for him to return for almost a week, we were left in a dire predicament. We only had a little bit of money left to live on, and we were running low on groceries. Moreover, all of us were very troubled and didn't know what to do.

At that point, our mother realized, she could wait no longer and had no choice, but to go out looking for him. Some Slovak neighbors, who knew our father, told our mother that he might be in the Bronx where he was known to have some friends. They gave our mother and Ronnie, directions as to which neighborhood he might have gone to. Then our mother and Ronnie took a train to the South Bronx, to start searching for our father. Not knowing where to go, Ronnie found a police officer and tried to explain their problem to him in broken English as best she could. It was raining and starting to get dark, so the police officer suggested they should wait, until the following morning to continue their search.

They didn't have any place to spend the night and were low on funds. Fortunately, the police officer was able to find them an unlocked empty apartment. As he was going off duty, he told them to spend the night there. He told them that he would return the next morning, to continue helping them to find our father. After having locked themselves in the empty apartment, they tried to fall asleep on the bare floor. However, neither one of them were able to sleep. They were nervous and frightened being in an empty apartment in a strange neighborhood. Instead, they huddled together and recited 'The Holy Rosary' anxiously waiting for the long night to end.

Meanwhile, when our mother and Ronnie didn't return home later that night, all of us were very worried that something terrible might have happened to them. Tony was left in charge of the rest of us while they were gone. It was a difficult and tearful night. Tony did his best, trying to reassure us that everything would be all right.

The following morning, our mother and Ronnie were very relieved when the police officer returned to the apartment. He was a very compassionate and thoughtful person, as he even brought with him a bottle of milk and some pastry for their breakfast. Shortly after that, he escorted them to police headquarters where, strangely enough, our father was being held. He had been arrested for being drunk and disorderly. After explaining their sad situation to the police, our father was released to them, and all three were able to return back home to Hastings. Once they arrived back home, Tony and the rest of us were overjoyed to see them again.

The War in Europe Begins

It was now September, 1939. I remember one particular late afternoon, when we were all at home listening to a Polish radio station. The announcer was crying hysterically, Germany was invading Poland and slaughtering thousands of Polish people. Our mother was extremely upset and crying because all those poor people were being killed for no reason. The War in Europe had now started, as Britain and France declared War on Germany. We were all very worried about how many more people would be killed in Europe.

Moving to the Bronx and Continuous Hardships

Shortly after that, my father lost his job at the factory. I'm pretty sure that he was terminated because of his constant tardiness and absences, due to his drinking binges. At about the same time, now that the widow had passed away, her heirs demanded that we begin paying rent for the apartment, which we were living in. With our father unemployed and unable to find any new employment in town, we could no longer afford to stay in Hastings.

Our father then decided to move to Wilkins Avenue in the South Bronx, where we became superintendents of a large apartment building. We lived in the basement and managed the care and cleaning of the building. The arrangement was that we lived rent-free, along with receiving a small salary for maintaining the building.

Our duties were to sweep and mop the halls, collect the garbage through the dumbwaiter every evening, and haul it out to the sidewalk. When it snowed, we had to shovel the walkways. In addition, we shoveled the coal into the furnace for the heat and hot water of the building, along with disposing of the ashes daily. We all shared in the duties with our mother. Eventually, our father was able to find a job in the city as a factory worker.

My sisters and I attended the P.S. 54 Grammar School on Intervale Avenue in the Bronx, which was about three long blocks from our home. We were still the oldest and tallest in our classes as we had a lot to learn because we had a late start. The kids still made fun of us, I remember always being picked on and getting into a lot of fights. They called us refugees, greenhorns, and stupid Polacks, which greatly upset us. After a while, we decided to try to ignore them and no longer give them any credence. Eventually, they stopped the teasing and the name calling.

There was one time, that I had a fight with a black school kid named Alphonse. He would often bully and pick on me. Finally, I had enough, so one afternoon after class, I challenged him. I was able to wrestle him down to the ground and made him give up. The next morning, thinking that I would now pick on him, Alphonse approached me with a bunch of his friends. They told me, if I didn't leave him alone, they would all gang up on me and beat me up. After that, though, I wasn't picked on or bullied anymore, and we even became friends.

On our way home from school for lunch each day, we passed by a particular restaurant and peered in the windows, where they had white tablecloths on all of the tables in the dining room. The waiters were all dressed in their uniforms, and the men dressed in their business suits were having their lunch. I thought these people must be very rich to be able to eat in such a fine restaurant. I imagined how nice it would be, if we could afford to bring our mother to such a nice restaurant to have dinner and how thrilled she would be.

A few months after moving from Hastings to the Bronx, our father still continued his heavy drinking. One night, our mother was dreadfully ill and in bed with the flu. Our father had arrived home drunk, reeking of alcohol and cigarettes. He wanted to talk, which was what he was in the habit of doing. He ordered our mother to get out of bed, and forced her to sit, and listen to him. His voice became louder and louder as he became more verbally abusive. He wouldn't let our mother rest. By then, we were all awake. We knew that, we had to get her away from him. We then bundled her up with warm clothes and took her out to the street, hoping that our father hadn't followed us. Luckily, he had not.

We just walked up the street, not knowing what to do, or where to go for help. Eventually, we went into the hallway of a nearby apartment building and waited there for a while. Our mother soon started to shake and whimper, so we huddled around her as best we could to keep her warm. Anything was better than going back to him. By then, we were all crying and afraid, thinking that she might die and leave us with him. After a while, we returned home praying to God that our father had fallen asleep. Fortunately, he had. We put our mother to bed, and we crept into ours being very quiet because we didn't want to wake our father. Thankfully, our mother's health improved a few days later.

Our first Christmas in America, found us living in the basement of the apartment building in the Bronx. It was not a very joyous, traditional Christmas as we didn't have a Christmas tree or decorations. Of course, there weren't any Christmas gifts. However, we did go to church to celebrate the Christmas Mass. After coming home, we had a traditional Slovak dinner in the late afternoon, which our mother prepared. Then after dinner, we listened to Christmas carols on the radio.

After moving to the Bronx, Tony was able to find a job working nights at a factory in Manhattan. He came home early in the morning. Usually, he brought home some apples, which he would eat before going to bed. He always just ate the center of the apples and left the rest. Then I would finish eating what was left of them. Sometimes Tony gave me some money to buy used comic books. I think at that time, they were about a penny apiece. In those days, we called them 'funny books.' We both enjoyed reading them. I think the comic books helped both Tony and me to learn our new language more quickly. Once we had read them, I traded them with some of my friends.

Tony Leaves Home

As time passed, our brother, Tony, was forced to move out of our apartment because of the frequent confrontations, he had with our father. Tony was not intimidated by him like we were. There was an occasion, one Saturday night, when our father came home after a night of drinking. He got into a heated argument with Tony, which almost led to blows between them. Then our father left, saying that he was going to the Police Department to report that Tony had physically attacked him. Our mother was very fearful, that Tony might be put in jail because of our father's false accusations.

Therefore, Tony quickly gathered up some of his clothes, and told our mother, he would go to stay with a friend of his that he worked with, who had his own apartment. Fortunately, he was able to continue living there and split the rent with his friend. He was still working in the factory where he earned enough money to live on. Whenever he could, he visited our mother when our father was not at home. Occasionally, when Tony was able to, he gave our mother some money.

With Tony gone, we no longer received any part of his salary, which he used to contribute to the household. Now my sister, Ronnie, was forced to leave school at the age of fifteen to find a job and earn some money. She went to work looking after two young children, while their parents who owned a bakery managed their store. They often gave Ronnie all kinds of bread and cakes to bring home to us, which we really needed and enjoyed. Ronnie and my mother, both shared, all the burdens and hardships that we encountered.

Continuously on the Move

For the next three years, we constantly moved from one apartment building to another, still working as superintendents. All in all, we probably moved six or seven times, all over the Bronx, always changing schools. We went from Wilkins Avenue to Jennings Street, Freeman Street, Prospect Avenue, Simpson Street, and a few other neighborhoods. I never understood, at that time, why we moved so often. Apparently, after a few months, my father would get an advance from the landlord, where we lived, and then we quickly moved somewhere else. The only good thing, about us moving to so many different neighborhoods, was I got to know a lot of kids. After a while, no matter where I went in the Bronx, I always knew someone.

I remember one particular day, when I was walking along Southern Boulevard, which was up the street from where we lived on Simpson Street. At that time, I was eleven years old, and it seemed, I was always hungry. While walking, I passed by a deli with an open air window, where there were hot dogs cooking on the flat grill. 'Oh,' how good they smelled. I wished that I had some money, but I didn't. In those days, you could buy a hot dog for around ten cents, a soda, and crinkle cut French fries for a nickel each. Unfortunately, I never had twenty cents.

During those dark and difficult times, we all felt that we were looked down upon by people. We were very poor, and there was no one to help us, except ourselves. We hadn't realized, at that time, financial help was available from state agencies, churches, and other charitable organizations. However, no one ever gave us that information, so we never thought to seek any help. The few relatives that we had were living in Westfield, Massachusetts, but they never bothered to keep in touch with any of us.

Our Mother's Marital Strife

My mother was very unhappy and frustrated with my father because of his constant alcohol abuse, his womanizing, and his inability to keep a job. When he did work, he often spent his salary on drinking, and my mother wouldn't see any of it. Sometimes he even managed to obtain our payment from the landlord for maintenance of the building, which he would spend getting drunk. He would go on drinking binges for several days, leaving us with hardly any money for food. When he was home with us, we tried to stay out of his way, especially when he was drinking. When he would first start to drink, he was somewhat sociable, but the more he drank, his demeanor changed, and he became very mean. Our life was nothing, like my mother pictured it would be, once we reached America.

Even though, life was very difficult for us while living in Czechoslovakia, we were all much happier there, than we were now. I'll never understand, how our father could treat us the way he did. After all the things, our mother went through while living in Czechoslovakia: all the hardships that she had to endure, giving birth to his children, and doing everything as best she could to raise them without him being there. She struggled for almost nine long years, and finally came to America, dreaming of a better life, only to find that her life was now a living hell.

Chapter 5:

THE WAR YEARS

World War II Begins

After the Japanese bombing of Pearl Harbor on December 7th, 1941, the United States declared War on Japan. Within a few days, Germany declared War on the United States. We now had to defend ourselves on two fronts. By this time, Hitler had conquered almost all of Europe and had invaded Russia, inflicting heavy losses on the Russian Armed Forces. Everyone was worried that Hitler might succeed in conquering Russia, and if he did, what that might mean for America. Ronnie always brought home the New York Daily News. It showed the map of the advances of the Japanese and Nazis forces, which I kept track of from day to day. Every evening, my family and I listened to the radio hoping to hear good news about the War and our servicemen.

John is Drafted into the Army

My brother, John, had married a Slovak girl named Mary, in November of 1941. They lived in an apartment on East 73rd Street in Manhattan. Less than a year later, just after the birth of their first son, John Jr., John, at twenty-two years of age, was drafted into the Army. He was processed at Fort Dix, New Jersey, and he finished his basic training in South Carolina. Then he was transported to San Francisco, where he boarded a ship and was assigned to serve with the American Forces in New Caledonia, which was a group of French islands in the South Pacific. While he was there, he received additional training as a B.A.R. rifleman

(Browning Automatic- Rifle.) Upon completion of his training, he was assigned to the newly formed New England Division of the 43rd Infantry.

From New Caledonia, the 43rd Division took part in their first military action on the island of Guadalcanal, helping the Marines in driving the Japanese forces from the island. While on Guadalcanal, John received a letter from his wife, Mary. She wrote saying, that she saw his picture in the Daily News, and he was wearing a Marine uniform, but she thought he was in the Army. John wrote back informing her, that the reason he was dressed as a Marine was because the Army didn't have any more of their uniforms, but the Marines had more than enough of theirs.

Now five years, after coming to America to seek safety from serving in the military in Czechoslovakia, John found himself on the other side of the world serving in the U.S. Army Infantry fighting the Japanese Forces, in the hot and steamy island jungles of the South Pacific. In the following months and years, he served and saw combat in the Russell Islands, New Georgia, New Guinea, and the Northern Solomon Islands. The 43rd Division was also greatly involved with combat operations on Luzon in the Philippines, and after months of fighting they achieved the final liberation of the island. John was infected with malaria several times while serving in the South Pacific. He was treated for malaria the first time in Australia, and then he was treated in New Zealand for his second bout of malaria. As was customary, he was given R&R following his treatment both times. Then when he was once again fit for active duty, he returned to his outfit.

Shortly after John was drafted into the Army, his wife, Mary, moved in with her parents, who lived in a Manhattan apartment. She then went to work in a defense plant in Brooklyn, along with our sister, Rose, who had quit school. Rose was now sixteen years old, but lied saying she was eighteen in order to get the job. They never bothered to question her age as they needed anyone, who was willing to work. Our mother took care of John and Mary's son, Johnny, who lived with us, during that time, as both of Mary's parents also worked. During those years, there was an explosion of jobs to be had. It seemed that every able-bodied man and woman was working in some sort of a defense plant, helping manufacture everything from ships and planes, to the smallest items to help in the War effort. Meanwhile, the grandparents cared for the children.

It was a time, when women were no longer 'stay at home moms' while their husbands served in the military defending our country. They were asked to fill the needs, which men used to do in all types of work. There were posters, such as 'Rosie the Riveter' and movie newsreels, depicting women working in all sorts of factories and shipyards.

Separating from Our Father

After four years in early 1943, when I was eleven, we all decided that we had enough of living with our father. We could no longer tolerate his constant drinking and verbal abuse. He was just impossible to live with. Ronnie and Rose were both now working, so we were able to afford to live on our own. One day, while our father was at work, we just up and left him. We moved to a fifth-floor apartment on Fox Street in the Bronx, where the rent was very affordable. We had gone from the basement to the top floor. The apartment had an ice box, and the ice needed to be replenished at least a couple of times a week. I remember going to the ice house, which was a few blocks away, and having to carry buckets of large blocks of ice back home, and up the five flights of stairs when the 'Ice Man' didn't deliver.

We no longer felt like second-class citizens. By now, all of us children were well versed in our new language as we had been taught how to read, write, and speak English. We were happy as we all got along well with each other, and there were no more arguments. Our household, once again, was nice and peaceful.

Tony is Drafted into the Army

In the spring of 1943, my brother, Tony, now twenty years of age, was drafted into the Army, which we had anticipated he would be. While he was in the process of completing his basic training at Fort Dix, New Jersey, he was able to come home one weekend on leave. He had put on some weight, and he looked great in his Army uniform. Before he left, our mother gave him a scapular (a cloth necklace worn by Catholics to show devotion) and told him that it would protect him from any harm.

By the summer of 1943, upon finishing his basic training, Tony volunteered to join the elite 2nd Ranger Battalion, which was formed for a special mission in the liberation of Europe. He was shipped to Tennessee to continue special training at Camp Forest, where three thousand volunteers took part in rigorous training. In the end, only five hundred were able to qualify. Tony was one of them. They formed the 2nd Ranger Battalion, which consisted of six companies: A, B, C, D, E, and F. When their training was completed in Tennessee, they were transported to Fort Pierce in Florida for amphibious training, before being shipped to England on the Queen Elizabeth. Once in England, his Battalion received special training from the British Commandos. Training included climbing high cliffs, going on long field marches, and learning hand-to-hand combat. They continued their training until the invasion of Europe was initiated.

Reconciliation with Our Father

By the fall of 1943, after we had been separated from and hadn't seen our father for eight months, he eventually found out where we lived, so he would often visit our mother. He told her how sorry he was for mistreating all of us, and that he was now a changed man. Our father promised to stop drinking, if only, we would give him a second chance and take him back. In fact, it was the only time, that I remember him giving me any spending money. I think he was trying to bribe me to show my mother that he was going to be different now.

Being as loving and forgiving as our mother was, she convinced us that maybe, we should try again to see if he really was sincere in not drinking anymore, and that he would try to get along with all of us. She was a devout Catholic, and she didn't believe in divorce or separation from one's spouse. After having been on our own for a while, we moved in with our father on Bryant Avenue, which was still in the Bronx and still on the top floor where the rent was always cheaper. The first few weeks that, he was living with us were relatively peaceful. However, as time went on, he returned to his old ways of drinking and verbal abuse. We all realized then, that he really hadn't changed at all.

After coming home from work and eating dinner, my father often gave me some money to fetch him a large pitcher of beer from the neighborhood bar. He would then sit in the kitchen and have my mother sit there with him. My father wanted a drinking buddy, but my mother wasn't a drinker. Nevertheless, she was forced to sit with him for hours on end and listen to his complaints about everything that, he thought was wrong in the world.

There was one time, when my sisters and I decided to play a joke on our father. We filled up one of his empty whiskey bottles with coffee. It looked very much like whiskey in color and we gave it to him. He was surprised and proceeded to drink from it. Our father wasn't at all pleased, when he discovered that it was just coffee and not whiskey. Of course, we were all standing there as he took his first sip and waited for his reaction, which was pretty much what we expected. We all got quite a laugh from it, but he didn't appreciate our joke.

While living on Bryant Avenue, I became friends with a couple of brothers in the neighborhood, who were about my age, around twelve or thirteen. I think, they were either Swedish or Norwegian as they both had platinum blond hair. After we had been friendly for some time, they invited me into their home to play some games. The day I went there, I was in for a shock. Their mother was walking around the apartment, with no clothes on. She was stark naked! I was very embarrassed, but the brothers said, she always, walked around like that during the warm summer months. They didn't seem to think that seeing their mother naked was a big deal. It was the first and last time, I went there. That was something totally foreign to me as no one in my family would ever think of doing something like that.

D-Day, June 6th, 1944

I remember coming home from school, in the late afternoon, on June 6th, 1944, and finding my mother sitting at the kitchen table. She was visibly shaken and upset as she held her Rosary beads in her hands and was praying. Meanwhile, she was sobbing with tears running down her cheeks. I asked her what had happened, and why was she crying? She said, she was listening to the radio and heard that the invasion of Europe was now underway. She was crying and praying for all the men and boys, who were being killed on the beaches of Normandy. Knowing that her son was among them made it more personal, and she prayed that God would spare his life.

A few days later, we received a telegram from the War Department informing us, that Tony had been seriously wounded during the assault at Normandy, but he was alive. All of us were very thankful to learn that he was alive. We were all praying for his recovery when a few days later, we received a second telegram from the War Department. This time, they wrote that Tony was now missing in action. Needless to say, we were all very upset upon reading the terrible news, but for some unknown reason, all of us seemed to feel that he was alright. Several days later, our mother said, she had a dream one night, and in it Jesus came to her, telling her not to worry because Tony was alive and well.

The Final Separation

By July of 1944, a month after D-Day, our main concern was Tony's welfare. We all took stock in our positive feelings and our mother's previous dream, although we still continued to hope and pray that Tony truly was alive and well. We were also very unhappy living with our father, realizing that he would never stop drinking. Therefore, we separated from him again. Back then, none of us knew that alcoholism was a disease, and without proper treatment it was almost impossible to overcome. Apparently, he wasn't capable of helping himself unless he sought professional help. Of course, he wasn't about to do that. It's a terrible addiction as often lives are ruined by it. Moreover, the drinker enjoys drinking and therefore, is in denial that drinking is a problem.

Having left him again, we moved to another part of the Bronx. Once again, we lived on the top floor of a five-story building on the corner of East 170th Street and Wilkins Avenue. This time, there was no going back, our father had been given another chance, and he had blown it. To this day about the only thing, which I can give him credit for was coming to America when he did and befriending the widow. If he hadn't, we would all probably have remained in Czechoslovakia. Therefore, we do have to thank him for that.

Always in need of more money, my mother went to work for a short time at night, cleaning offices in Manhattan, but it was just too much for her. She was forced to give it up because of her heart condition. After we left our father and were living on our own for a while, he would find our mother when she was out doing the shopping. Our father would always make a scene, arguing and yelling at her for leaving him. She would get very upset and was fearful of him. From then on, we made sure that she was never out alone, until he finally stopped coming around.

Life in the Bronx during the War

During the summer months, I hardly ever stayed indoors as there was nothing to do. There were no televisions or computers. I was always outside with the other kids playing some sort of game, coming in for supper, and then going outside again. I wouldn't return home, until it started to grow dark. Sometimes we played a game called Skelly. We would press orange or banana peels into soda or beer bottle caps. Then we slid them on the sidewalk, trying to get them as close as possible to the chalk line. It was a bit like shuffleboard. When we had money, for a few cents, we were able to buy Topps gum, which also included baseball cards. Then we flipped the cards with our friends, trying to win some of theirs to add to our collection. If we had a pink Spaldeen (a rubber ball, which was slightly smaller than a tennis ball) we played stoop ball and punch ball with our friends.

Everyone played with marbles in those days. There were the multi-colored ones, as well as the clear and the (metal) steelies. Once, I found an old single roller-skate, which I was able to use in the making of a scooter. I took the skate apart, nailed one part on the front of a two-by-four, and the second part on the end of it. Then I was able to find a wooden apple fruit box, and mounted it on the two-by-four, and put handles on it. That scooter was my pride and joy. I had it for the longest time, until the skates finally wore out.

On Saturday mornings, we went to the movies as it only cost about six cents. Not only that, but we received all sorts of free candy at the door. Sometimes they even gave us free comic books. Usually, we watched three movies along with cartoons. We pretty much spent the whole day there. They showed a lot of cowboy movies with Gene Autry, Roy Rogers and the Lone Ranger, along with Charlie Chan mysteries, and some Charlie Chaplin films.

In those days, when we bought a movie ticket, the number on the stub enabled us to win prizes. Many times, I had good luck winning. One time, I won a complete set of dishes. I was so excited that I didn't even finish watching the rest of the movies. I just wanted to bring them home to my mother. Therefore, I enlisted the aid of my three sisters, and we carried them home to show our mother what I had won. Of course, she was very happy to get a new set of dishes.

No one ever, gave me any money to spend. I had to go out and earn it, if I wanted to buy anything. During the Jewish holidays, I lit candles for the elderly Jewish ladies in their homes. Usually, they gave me a few cents for doing that. I also helped them carry their bags of groceries to their homes to earn some money.

Sometimes when I looked down into the storm grates on the street, I would see coins that people had lost. Then I fished for the coins by using a string with a weight on the end of it, along with some sticky chewing gum. It wasn't easy, but the trick was to get the coins to stick to the gum. Once it stuck, then I was able to hoist them up. If I was lucky enough to find a quarter, I felt like, I hit the jackpot!

As the War continued there were blackouts. During the blackouts, everyone had to shut off all the lights in their homes, along with making sure, the blackout shades were pulled down, and that the curtains were closed. Then the blackout wardens would come by to check the neighborhoods, making sure everyone complied. There were always scrap metal and paper drives to help the War effort. Whenever, we could afford to, we bought War Bonds. In our window, we had a small banner with two red stars, signifying, we had two members of our family serving in the military. We were extremely proud of both John and Tony.

During those years, many commodities were being rationed. You couldn't buy butter, sugar, or meat without ration stamps, and even then, those items were very limited. In place of butter, we all used what they called in those days, 'oleomargarine.' It was white in color, so you added and mixed in a light orange colored substance to make it look like butter. Even then, it never tasted like butter. What we missed most, was sugar as it was very hard to come by, even if you had ration stamps. Usually, the grocers only sold sugar to their best customers.

Some butcher stores even sold horse meat because of the shortage of beef and pork. Once, our mother bought some horse meat, but when we ate it, we didn't care for the taste, and we never had it again. All in all, not being able to buy meat didn't bother us much. Our mother prepared the same meals, which we always had in Czechoslovakia, consisting of a lot of non-rationed foods. There were never any shortages of fresh fruits, vegetables, and bread products.

The popular brands of cigarettes were nowhere to be found, but every so often I was able to buy my sister, Ronnie, some Pall Mall cigarettes from an older fellow, whom I knew. In those days, it seemed like everyone was smoking cigarettes. Some things you couldn't buy at all, such as women's silk stockings, the silk was used to make parachutes. If you owned a car, you were limited as to how much gasoline you were allowed to buy because that was rationed as well, unless you were part of the War effort.

We went to St. John's Church off Southern Boulevard every Sunday. Our prayers were for the War to end, and for all the soldiers to come home. Of course, we also specifically prayed for John and Tony to safely return home to us. Everyone was very patriotic, hoping and praying for the War to end. At that time, people were more polite and friendlier to one another. It just seemed that the country, as a whole was more unified in those days.

During the warm summer months, the people in the neighborhood gathered outside, and sat on the stoop of their buildings, and socialized. Others listened to their portable radios. Doing that, you were able to become acquainted with some of the neighbors on the block. On the real hot nights, some people even slept outside on their fire escapes. No one had air conditioners then, so no one wanted to spend any more time indoors than they needed to. We did have some electric fans, which helped to cool us off. During the day, we left all the windows and doors to our apartment open, which allowed the breeze to blow through to cool our rooms. If you lived on the top floor, your apartment would bake under the hot sun from the black tar-papered roof above. Back then, people didn't need to lock their doors during the day when they were at home. People also were able to walk the streets late at night, without fear of their safety.

Prisoner of War

It was several months after D-Day, in September of 1944, when we received a letter from Tony through the American Red Cross. We were all surprised and overjoyed to hear from him. He wrote in his letter, that he was okay, but he was a prisoner of War. We were told by the Red Cross, to write to him only in English, to make it very brief, and not to write anything about the War.

Germany Surrenders and Tony Returns Home

On May 8th, 1945, which was called V-E Day, it was announced in the newspapers and on the radio that, Germany had surrendered unconditionally. Thankfully, the War in Europe was finally over! Everyone was overjoyed. All three of my sisters went to Times Square to join in the celebration, along with thousands of other people. My mother and I remained at home, listening to the celebration on the radio. We were also very happy that, at last, Tony would be coming home. However, we still worried about the War in the Pacific, praying for it to end, and that John would soon be coming home as well.

Tony was liberated by the Russians from the prison camp in Dresden, Germany. Soon after, he was reunited with his outfit, and then he was sent to Paris for some much needed R&R. While in Paris, he decided to travel back to Czechoslovakia to visit our relatives before coming home. He wasn't sure, if he would ever get an opportunity to do that in the future. First he spent a few days, visiting our mother's sister, Agatha, in Prague. Then he continued on his way to Slovakia, to visit our relatives there. Upon arriving in Hincovce at our uncle, Gustin's, house, he knocked on the door, and our aunt, Katrina, opened it. She was startled and very apprehensive as she didn't recognize Tony, so she called Gustin, and told him, there was a soldier at the door. When Gustin came to the door, he also didn't recognize Tony. It was only when, Tony asked, "aren't you going to offer me a drink?" in Slovak, that he finally recognized him. He was very surprised and thrilled to see Tony again.

During the War, we were unable to correspond with any of our relatives there, so no one knew anything about us. Of course, we in turn, didn't know anything about them either. Tony told Uncle Gustin about everything, which had happened since the time we left Czechoslovakia, and that John was also in the Army currently serving in the South Pacific. Our uncle was very sad and sorry, to learn of the hardships and the abuse that our father had inflicted on our mother as he loved her very much. You can hardly imagine, how they felt seeing Tony. He left Czechoslovakia as a teenager and now, he came back as a man and a soldier, who had participated in the liberation of Europe. He was quite the celebrity, all of the people in the villages of Hincovce and Trstany celebrated his return. Then he went to Zdiar, to visit all of our remaining relatives there and they, too, were surprised and very happy to see him again.

When he arrived home in the summer of 1945, we barely recognized him. He had lost a great amount of weight. Being in the prison camps had taken a heavy toll on him, both physically and psychologically. You could tell that he had been through a great deal. The Army then sent him to Lake Placid, New York for about a month to get some additional and much needed R&R.

The Battle at Pointe Du Hoc

It was only at the end of the War in 1945, when Tony came home, that we learned what had really happened to him. He said, the Rangers were never informed as to what their mission was going to be while training. However, the fact that they were climbing high cliffs while in England gave them a pretty good idea that, it was probably going to be very dangerous. It was only, just before they were getting ready to attack, that they were told the target was Pointe Du Hoc in Normandy. Tony having left the shores of France, in February of 1939, and coming to America as a teenager, was now informed that he would be going back to the beaches of France to take part in the Allied Liberation of Europe.

While growing up in Trstany, when Tony was about fifteen years old, he went to see a Gypsy fortune teller. There were always a number of Gypsies frequently traveling through our area in Czechoslovakia. He asked her, how long, was he going to live. The fortune teller told him, that he wouldn't die until he was in his late forties. I think he really believed her, and he felt that no harm would come to him while he was serving in the Army, as he was only in his early twenties. In the days before the attack, doubt set in and Tony couldn't help, but wonder if what the fortune teller had told him was true, or if he would be killed.

He told us that in the early morning, of June 6th, 1944, the companies D, E, and F of the 2nd Ranger Battalion were finally informed, that they would have to scale the 120-foot high cliffs on Pointe Du Hoc in Normandy. Their mission was to knock out the six huge 155mm guns, which were entrenched in the bunkers on the top of the cliffs. Tony was a member of E company. Those guns gave the Germans command of both the Utah and Omaha Beaches, which posed a tremendous threat to the landing of the

Allied forces. Pointe Du Hoc was a small tableland jutting out into the English Channel, like the letter 'V.' The military invasion planners called Pointe Du Hoc, 'target number one.' Companies A, B, and C of the 2nd Ranger Battalion, along with the 5th Ranger Battalion were to attack on a different part of Omaha Beach. Once their mission there was complete, they were to join the Ranger companies of D, E, and F on Pointe Du Hoc.

After a hearty breakfast of pancakes and strong coffee, which was supposed to reduce the possibility of sea sickness, they left their landing ships. After being loaded onto their landing barges, Companies D, E, and F were lowered into the black and choppy waters of the English Channel. Tony said, the Rangers were set to arrive at Pointe Du Hoc at six a.m., but they were blown off course, due to the high winds and the rough four-foot high waves. While being in their landing barges, waiting to reach the shore, Tony said that a number of his fellow Rangers were holding Rosary beads and praying just like he was.

When they finally corrected their course and arrived at Pointe Du Hoc, they were more than forty-five minutes late. They had now lost the element of surprise, and the Germans were there waiting for them. The Naval fire from the American Destroyers drove the Germans away from the top of the cliffs and into their bunkers. However, once the shelling stopped, the Germans came out of their bunkers and were ready to fire on the Rangers, who were about to land on the beach below.

Finally, as they reached the beach and disembarked, the Rangers were met with a barrage of hand grenades, devastating machine gun, and enormous rifle fire from above. As soon as some of the Rangers had landed on the beach, they used rocket-fired grappling hooks to secure rope ladders on the top of the cliffs, and then they quickly tried to scale to the top. While some of the Rangers were climbing the rope ladders, the Germans dislodged them causing them to fall to their deaths. Tony was able to make it to the top okay. Once the remaining Rangers, reached the top of the cliffs, they pushed the Germans back. They were amazed to see the guns, which they were sent to destroy, weren't there. Instead, they found large wooden poles placed in the bunkers to give the illusion of artillery guns.

Realizing, that the real guns couldn't be too far away, the Rangers drove inland for about a mile and found the bunkers and the guns abandoned, with not a German soldier in sight. Then the Rangers planted their thermit grenades and rendered the guns useless. Tony said that, while some of the Rangers destroyed the 155mm guns, he and some of the others took cover in a German bunker as the Navy Destroyers were once again shelling the area. The bombardment was so intense, that one of the Rangers became shell shocked.

On June 7th, the Germans counter-attacked Tony's position a number of times, but they were always beaten back. Eventually, the German's were able to overrun it with an overwhelming force, although they sustained heavy casualties. After fierce fighting, Tony was wounded by a grenade fragment in his shoulder. Then a German soldier appeared, out of nowhere, knocking Tony's machine gun from his hands and held a bayonet to his throat. Tony immediately, raised his arms up in the act of surrender, fearing for his life, waiting for the thrust of the bayonet. He thought, surely, his life was going to end. At that moment, Tony said, they looked into each other's eyes, for what seemed like an eternity, and thankfully the German soldier lowered his bayonet from Tony's neck, sparing his life. Instead, he was taken prisoner, along with some other fellow

Rangers. As his life had been spared, Tony now wondered if the Gypsy fortune teller had truly foreseen his future.

Once the Rangers had completed their mission on Pointe Du Hoc, they were to wait for the remaining three companies, A, B, and C of the 2nd Ranger Battalion and the 5th Ranger Battalion to join them. None of them, though, were able to help the Rangers on Pointe Du Hoc because they were pinned down by heavy German forces on Omaha Beach. It took several days for those Rangers, along with the 116th Infantry to finally break through and relieved the surviving Rangers of companies, D, E, and F on Pointe Du Hoc.

The mission was a great success, but with a tremendous loss of life. Out of two hundred and twenty-five Rangers, who took part in the assault on Pointe Du Hoc, only ninety had survived. It was the greatest loss of life that, the American military suffered in a single battle on the assault of Europe. Later, the 2nd Ranger Battalion was awarded the Presidential Unit Citation, and the French Croix de Silver Gilt Star. Many military historians called the assault on

Pointe Du Hoc, the bloodiest action of World War II in the European Theatre of War.

Tony was a prisoner of War for almost a year. During that time, Tony said that he was shipped to a number of different prison camps in Germany as the Allies continued to make progress in the liberation of Europe. His wound healed up in the prison camps, but some of the shrapnel still remained in his shoulder. It caused him some discomfort for the rest of his life. The last prison camp, he was confined to was in Dresden, Germany, where he was liberated by the Russian Armed Forces at the close of the War.

Upon coming home, he never spoke much about the time, which he spent in the prison camps because he didn't want to upset our mother. However, he did mention once to our brother, John, that he was confined in a barracks with British and American prisoners while the Russian prisoners were in a separate barracks, strictly by themselves. The Germans had a tremendous hatred of the Russians. Every so often, during the cold winter months, the German guards would order a number of Russian prisoners to strip off their clothes and spend the night outside of their barracks in the frigid cold. They were seen huddling together in a group, trying to keep warm from one another's body heat. Tragically, due to the extreme exposure, some of them froze to death. Thankfully, they never did that to the British or American prisoners.

Army Career

After his discharge, Tony tried to find a job, but he didn't have any experience in any trade or profession, and at that time jobs were hard to find. Therefore, he decided to re-enlist and retained his former rank in the Army. He was sent to Germany and served a number of tours there. He eventually made the decision to make the Army his career as all he ever knew was soldiering, which he was happy with.

Around that time, we started to see a lot of new and old faces in the neighborhood because all of the servicemen were being discharged. Many of them were reunited with their families. Things were starting to change as all the men, who had been discharged, were looking for work and trying to find places to live.

The Melting Pot

During and after the War, growing up in the Bronx was quite an experience. It was a great place to grow up in, and I had a good time living there. I always had a lot of friends, and I met a lot of kids of different nationalities: Jewish, Spanish, Italian, Polish, German, Irish, pretty much a little of everything. The Bronx was truly a melting pot. Having made friends with kids of all different nationalities, I was introduced to all kinds of cuisine: pickled herring, bagels and lox, all kinds of pasta dishes, rice and beans, and of course, we all liked the Jewish deli food.

There was an open-air market on Jennings Street. In addition, there was a great variety of grocery stores and numerous fruit stands, where you could buy all sorts of fresh fruits, vegetables, along with all kinds of meats, and dairy products. It was a very busy shopping center in that area. You had to be careful, whenever you bought fruit because if you weren't watching the fruit merchant, he had been known to throw in some bad fruit. You also could buy delicious sour pickles from Jake, the pickle man, who fished them out of a large wooden barrel with his bare hand.

There was the popular Mager's Bakery on Wilkin's Avenue, which sold delicious Jewish rye bread, their famous hard rolls, along with all kinds of coffee cakes, and pastries. We always stopped there, after coming home from church on Sunday. Nearby on the Boston Post Road was Annie's Jewish Deli, known for their great hot pastrami and corned beef sandwiches, along with their tasty potato salad. Of course, there were always the delicious hot dogs covered with sauerkraut and spicy mustard. It seemed that there was a candy store on every street corner in the neighborhood, where you could buy egg creams and milk shakes, which we called 'malteds,' and all sorts of candy, and comic books. There were also the street vendors with their push carts, selling delicious jelly candied apples and roasted sweet potatoes.

Everyone knew and frequented Melman's Drug Store. Mr. Melman, the pharmacist, was also the appointed neighborhood doctor. He gave out medical advice and answered questions. If you had something in your eye, he removed it for you. He applied Iodine on your cuts and bruises, and he treated you for a number of other things as well.

We lived next door to an Italian woman named Mary Patti, whose husband had just passed away. She had two children: a son named Tony, and a younger daughter named Gracie. Eventually, I became very friendly with her son as were both fourteen. Tony and I were inseparable, becoming best friends for a number of years. I also picked up a few of his bad habits, such as smoking cigarettes. One afternoon, while we were on the roof of our apartment building smoking cigarettes, Tony's mother caught us. She grabbed Tony by the neck and dragged him back into their apartment, where she proceeded to hit him with a broomstick. I was there and witnessed the whole incident. Tony was screaming and yelling, trying to get away from her, running from room to room, but was unable to do so. His sister, Gracie, all the while, was chasing after the both of them. She was very upset and kept begging her mother to please stop hitting her brother, but their mother wouldn't let up. After the beating, I asked Tony if she hurt him, and he said "Nah, I just yelled and screamed to make her stop hitting me, but she didn't really hurt me."

Looking back now, it seems that, I always managed to attract friends, who were a little brash, bold, and challenging. Perhaps, this was because I was fairly conservative and quiet, so I guess it's true when they say that opposites attract. If we were on Wilkins Avenue doing something, and if Tony's mother needed him, she would yell out for him from an open window on the top floor of the building. You would hear this loud bellowing voice, yelling, "Nino," "Nino," throughout the whole neighborhood. Tony's mother was a terrific cook. She made the best spaghetti and meatballs, I've ever tasted. Sometimes Tony came to our apartment, and we ate cold ham and the potato salad that my mother made, which he enjoyed a lot.

My mother and Tony's mother became very friendly. They visited one another quite often, and conversed in broken English. It was just amazing, that even though, they had a difficult time conversing they were still able to communicate. She was a very nice woman, and I liked her a lot. As it was the Sicilian custom, being a widow, she always wore black, until she remarried years later. Both of our mothers had a lot in common with each other, since each had been born in a foreign country, had immigrated to America, and had endured a great deal of hardship during their lifetime.

Every so often, usually on Sunday, a number of Tony's relatives would come to visit his mother, and he had a lot of them. She cooked all kinds of food for their dinner. I was amazed one day, when Tony invited me in to see all the food, which his mother had prepared. There was tomato sauce, pasta, meatballs, sausage, bracciole, lasagna, eggplant, broccoli rhab, spinach with olive oil and garlic. In addition, there was a variety of cooked vegetables, Italian bread, melons, and all kinds of fruit, along with wine and soda, spread before my eyes on the dining room table. It was an Italian custom to just spend the whole afternoon, socializing and eating. To me, it was just unbelievable that people could eat so much at one sitting.

Being the youngest and a teenager, and having to live with four females, proved to be a little difficult at times. We had our share of differences, but never anything serious. My sisters had each other for female company. What I missed the most, was not having an older male influence during my teen years as I really didn't have a father. Tony was eight years older than me, and John was ten years older, so we really didn't have much in common. Unfortunately, I never saw them that much because of the War.

Trying to Earn Some Money

While attending the Herman Ridder Junior High School, I clowned around a lot in class because I was bored, and I didn't have any sense of direction. A few of my friends and I would cut class and go across the street to Crotona Park. While there, we played handball or basketball, and then later, we returned to school. I think that, I tried to cover up my feelings of insecurity by doing all that, which I realize now was very foolish of me.

It was also during that time, in 1945, that my sister, Mary, left school at age sixteen and went to work at the Horn & Hardart Bakery in the Parkchester section of the Bronx. She eventually became the manager of the store and received an increase in her salary. We now had three incomes coming into the family, and things were beginning to look much brighter.

I still went to school, but I never really took it seriously. I also worked part-time to earn a few dollars by shining shoes with my friend, Tony. We even went on Broadway, a few times on the weekends, but we were chased away by the adult shoe-shine people, who had their spots and didn't want any competition. Other weekends, we would hitch a ride on the rear of a trolley car with our shoe shine boxes on the back of our shoulders, and go to West Farms Road to try to earn some money there by shining shoes.

We cut school for a few days, and sold newspapers in the 42nd Street subway station when the Daily News workers went on strike. We always did very well, buying the papers for two cents from the Daily News outlet and selling them for five or ten cents, but the strike didn't last, too long. In addition, occasionally I worked for Charlie's Linoleum Store on Wilkin's Avenue after school and on Saturdays with a friend of mine called Patsy, helping to install linoleum. As I got older, I worked some Saturdays for a fruit store with Tony, delivering fruit on a bicycle. I realized then, that at some point in my life I, too, would go into business for myself.

Always Something to Do

During the school summer vacation, whenever we weren't working, we met at the corner candy store on Boston Post Road and Charlotte Street and planned our day. There was Tony, Herbie, Izzy, Heshy, Louie, Marty, and the brothers Tony and Patsy, along with a lot of other kids in the neighborhood. There was always something to do, but most of the time no one had any money to spend. Whenever, one of us did have some spending money, we bought some ice cream or candy, which we shared with the rest of the guys.

If we went downtown into Manhattan, we would sneak onto the subway. At that time, it was only a nickel, but it was more fun to sneak on. We waited, until just before the train was ready to close the doors, then we jumped over the turnstiles, and made a mad dash for it.

Occasionally, we hitched a ride on the back of a trolley car, and went to the RKO Chester Movie House on West Farms Road to see a movie. The trolley car drivers didn't like us hitching a ride on the back of the cars. Sometimes the driver chased us, but as soon as he got back on, we jumped back on again, too. One day, as Tony and I were hitching a ride, the trolley stopped, and we hung on. Then suddenly, out of nowhere, the driver grabbed Tony and gave him a couple of good whacks before Tony was able to get away. I was fortunate, I ran away while that was happening, but after that anytime we hitched a ride, we were very vigilant.

Other times we would sneak into the Bronx Zoo, by climbing over the fence, and spend the whole day there. Whenever, the New York Giants were scheduled to play at the Polo Grounds Stadium, we went there and waited until the people stood up, and began to sing the National Anthem, and then we climbed over the wall and watched them play baseball. At the Boston Post Road Movie Theatre, one of us bought a ticket to get in, and then opened the side door, so that the rest of us could sneak in.

There were always all sorts of things to keep us busy. We played johnny on the pony, ringo-leevio, and ping-pong in the P.S. 61 school gym. Sometimes we pitched pennies against a wall, and the one with the penny closest to the wall was the winner. We also played basketball and softball in the schoolyard and other games as well. In the wintertime, when it snowed we went up on an apartment building roof, and we threw snowballs at the girls walking below.

Aside from doing things like that, we really weren't bad kids, perhaps a bit mischievous and rowdy at times, but never doing anything bad or destructive. We always tried to stay out of trouble. My mother, though, was sometimes very concerned about me. I tried to reassure her, that I would never give her any cause to worry about me, as she had more than her share of things to worry about. I wouldn't be much of a son, if I caused her any unnecessary concern.

In those days, there weren't many cars on the streets, so sometimes on the weekends we played stickball. All you needed was a pink Spaldeen ball and a broomstick. It was a great deal of fun. We played teams from other neighborhoods and bet against them, along with some of the adults, who watched us.

Time with My Family

Sometimes my mother, sisters, and I enjoyed going to Crotona Park on the weekend, which was just up the street from us. Our mother brought along a picnic lunch of sandwiches and potato salad. We always had a good time, getting some fresh air and sunshine while listening to music on our portable radio. Then we would walk around, and later we took a rowboat out on the lake, which was located within the park.

Other times during the summer, we went to Orchard Beach. Our mother made all sorts of sandwiches, which we brought with us. As the beach was quite a distance away, we had to take both the subway and the bus to get there. Once there, we spent time lying on the blanket on the hot sand while enjoying the sun, and then we would go into the water to cool off.

On one very hot Sunday, in July of 1945, my family and I decided to go to Orchard Beach. After lying on the blanket on the hot sand for a while, Mary and I decided to wade into the cool water. I slowly walked in, until it was up to my waist, and then I stood there for a few minutes. Suddenly, I felt the sand beneath me give way, and I sank over my head. Not knowing how to swim, I swallowed a lot of salt water, and was thrashing around with my arms, trying to get back on solid ground, but to no avail. As I sank below the surface of the water several times, and continued to swallow the salt water, I panicked thinking, I was going to drown. It was then, that I saw my short life flash before me. Finally, my sister, Mary, realized that I was in serious trouble. Then she grabbed my arm and pulled me to safety. It was biggest scare of my young life!

Around that time, my sister, Ronnie, had a job working in Manhattan. She took the subway on Freeman Street to work every morning. Generally, she always sat in a certain car on the subway, seeing the same faces, over and over again. One day a woman who was sitting near Ronnie, approached her and said, "You know, I've been riding this subway for quite a while, and I see you almost every day. I can't help, but notice that every time I see you, your hands are in your pocketbook and you keep moving your fingers all the time. Just what is it that, you're doing with them?" Ronnie looked at her, reached into her pocketbook, pulled out her Rosary beads, and said to her, "I recite The Holy Rosary."

There were times, when Ronnie didn't bother to take an umbrella with her in the morning as she went off to work. Some days late in the afternoon, when she was due to come home, it was pouring rain. Then I took my umbrella, walked down to the Freeman Street subway station, and waited there for her, along with the other people, who were also holding umbrellas and waiting. As she walked down the subway stairs, and saw me, she waved and gave me a big smile. I felt like a knight in shining armor, rescuing her from the pouring rain.

Japan Surrenders and John Returns

With the liberation of the Philippines, John's division, the 43rd played a major role in the fact that, the War was nearing its end. During the course of the War in the South Pacific, the 43rd was involved in three hundred seventy days of heavy combat with the Japanese Army and suffered six thousand twenty-six casualties. After all the hostilities ended in the Philippines, the United States military was amassing and training troops there for the invasion of the Japanese mainland. Still, the Japanese military government refused to surrender unconditionally, and they vowed to fight to the last man in defense of their homeland. The Allies feared that, the assault on the Japanese mainland would cost the military close to a million American casualties.

It was then, that the United States was forced to make the tragic decision to drop the Atomic bomb on the Japanese city of Hiroshima. The bomb completely destroyed the city, and killed more than two hundred thousand Japanese civilians. However, it took the additional Atomic bombing of Nagasaki, and hundreds of thousands of civilian casualties before the Japanese military finally surrendered unconditionally, and all military hostilities ended. On August 16th, 1945, V-J Day, the War in the Pacific, at last, was over! John and all the troops would be coming home.

Upon hearing of the Atomic bombing of Nagasaki and Hiroshima, everyone was devastated to learn of the tremendous number of Japanese civilians, who had perished. It was a pity that America had to resort to such means to end the War.

World War II Ends

We were now at peace on both fronts. Finally, World War II was over! Everyone was celebrating the good news. All of us thanked

God, for bringing both Tony and John safely back home to us. Our family once again would be whole.

At War's end, John was transported by ship to San Francisco. He was still infected with yet another bout of malaria, so he was flown to Fort Dix, New Jersey where he was treated for the disease. Then he was discharged from the Army. He had been away from his home and family for almost three years and during that time, he had served on various islands all over the South Pacific. Once Mary's job in the factory ended, and John returned home, both of them joined their son, Johnny, at our home, as he was already living with us. They continued living with us in the Bronx for a short time, until they could find a place of their own. Vacant apartments were very difficult to find because of all the servicemen, who were being discharged and returning home.

Chapter 6:

OUR FAMILY GROWS AND CHANGES

John

John was eventually able to find an apartment in Manhattan for himself and his family. He went searching for a job, but was unable to find anything, he really cared for. Therefore, he decided to open a little restaurant in the city. After a few months in business, he applied for a liquor license, but was turned down. After waiting for some time, he applied for a second time, and he was turned down again. John was very frustrated realizing, he would never be granted a permit because it seemed that he didn't know the right people. Since, he was unable to earn a worthwhile income, without the liquor license, he decided to sell the restaurant. Shortly after, when the new owner took possession of the restaurant, he was granted a liquor license. Apparently, the new owner must have known the right people.

Throughout the years, John worked at various jobs in the city, but never found any that suited him. Now having four children (Johnny, Michael, Jimmy, and Mary), John and his wife, Mary, decided to leave the city and moved to Nanuet, New York. John was able to get a VA mortgage to purchase a home there, and he also found a job at Lederly Pharmaceutical as a cafeteria helper. To supplement his income, he joined the New York 7th Regiment National Guard on Park Avenue in Manhattan, where he became the Mess Sergeant of the company kitchen. John also worked as a cook on the weekends for a local country club.

Rose

Once the War ended, there was no longer any need for the manufacturing of military equipment or products, so my sister, Rose, was let go, along with everyone else, who worked in the defense plants. With the help of our sister, Mary, Rose was able to get a job at a Horn & Hardart Bakery on Southern Boulevard in the Bronx. It was there, she met her future husband, Richard Lynch. He worked in his uncle's newsstand, which was right opposite the bakery where Rose worked. Richie constantly watched Rose through the store window. Once Richie became better acquainted with Rose, he told her, that he wanted to marry her. It seemed like it was love at first sight. They dated for a brief period, and then they were married in 1947. Rose and Richie moved in with his parents in an apartment on Bryant Avenue, a few miles away from where we lived.

With their marriage my mother had lost a daughter, but gained a son-in-law. Richie could be difficult at times, being short on patience, but he entered our lives when we needed someone. We all felt more secure, knowing that there was now someone to help us if need be. When Richie was a child, he was stricken with rheumatic fever, which left him with heart disease. That made him ineligible to serve in the Armed Forces, so he was home during the War years.

Within a short time, Rose gave birth to their first son, Kenny, and then later to another boy, whom they named Kevin. During that time, Richie's uncle decided to sell the newsstand, thus leaving Richie without a job. Then Richie and a good friend of his both decided to buy a local candy store in the Hunts Point Avenue section of the Bronx. The candy store seemed like a good investment. It was a gathering place for a large number of young people, located in a very busy area. However, when the Korean War broke out in

1950, the store began to suffer because the Army was drafting all the young men from the neighborhood. Before long, there was not enough business being generated in the store to make it worthwhile. It was then, that Richie's partner sold his share of the candy store to Richie. Despite the tremendous long hours and hard work, there was still not enough money coming in to make a decent living on. Sometimes on the weekends, my sister, Ronnie, and I tried to help him by working in the store, so that Richie could take a rest from the long hours, which he was putting in.

Rose now had two small children. At times, she felt tired out, due to the demands of being a mother with two little boys. To give Rose a rest on the weekends, I went to her apartment and picked up both boys in the morning and brought them back to our apartment, where our mother looked after them. I took them home again in the evening. The boys were very young, and it was a fairly long walk back to their home, so I carried one on my shoulders while the other one had to walk. Then I switched, and they took turns walking.

Realizing, that things weren't going to get much better with the store, Richie decided to sell it. Fortunately, he was able to find a job with a typesetting company in Manhattan as an apprentice compositor. Eventually, he became a journeyman compositor, earning more money. After a while, with the passing of his mother and his father now living in a convalescent home, Rose and Richie moved into the housing projects in the upper Bronx. The City of New York was building projects all over the city because of the housing shortage.

Mary

Mary was married shortly after Rose. She married Al Buchlein, a Postal worker. They moved to Rochelle Park in New Jersey, where they bought a new house. We weren't able to see her as often, as we would have liked because it was some distance away, and we didn't have a car. They eventually had two children, Neil, and Cathy.

Tony

In 1948, Tony came home on leave, after having re-enlisted in the Army. He told our mother, he was planning to marry a German girl named Irmgard, whom he had met while serving in Germany. Irmgard had recently given birth to their son, Bernd. Our mother gave Tony her blessing, and after a few weeks he returned to Germany and was married. While he was serving in Germany, we always received letters from him. On the envelopes we noticed, that from time to time, his rank would change from Sergeant to Corporal, and then back to Sergeant again. Knowing Tony, I believe it was because of the brawls, which he got into as he was very hot-tempered and quick to strike out.

My Teen Years

Once my sisters, Rose, and Mary, were married, we lost their income. To help with our finances, I left Roosevelt High School in my second year and started looking for full-time work. Now there was only me, Ronnie, and our mother left at home. I worked in Manhattan at Macy's on 34th Street and the U.S. Post Office at Christmas time. After that, I worked in several other places. Eventually, I went to work for the A&P Bakery on 138th Street and Bruckner Boulevard in the Bronx. It was a night position. My work hours were from eight p.m. at night to four a.m. in the morning. I unloaded freight cars filled with fifty-pound sacks of flour. It was very tiring work, but being young and strong it really didn't bother me that much.

There were four of us doing that work, and they called us 'the bull gang,' but I was hardly a bull. Being six-foot two and only weighing a hundred and fifty pounds, I was the skinniest guy of the bunch. I always had difficulty putting on weight. It was only, when I was in my early thirties that I weighed over two hundred pounds. Working those hours, I really didn't have much of a social life. Every day, it seemed like I would just get home, go to sleep, wake up in the early afternoon, have brunch, then a late dinner, and before I knew it, I was back at work.

My mother felt sorry for me because I doing such hard work. She wished, I could find something with less physical labor, but I didn't mind as the pay was pretty good. Our mother took half of our salaries and used it to run the household. She also made sure that we saved part of our salaries for the future. By now, the Korean War had escalated and a lot of my friends were being drafted into the Army. Some of them enlisted in the Air Force or the Navy, because they didn't want to be drafted into the Army or the Marines.

It was only a matter of time, before I would be receiving my draft notice. I was deeply worried about being drafted, because then there would just be Ronnie to care for our mother. When I voiced my concern to my brother, John, he recommended that I should join the National Guard. John was a member, and he told me, that if I joined then I would be deferred from the draft. Therefore, I joined the National Guard on Park Avenue in Manhattan, and as a member I was informed that there were a couple of mandatory requirements. The first was to attend the meetings, which were held every other Monday evening at the Armory. Every guardsman was also required to go, for two weeks every summer, to Camp Drum in upstate New York for training exercises.

Charlie's Poolroom

In those days on the weekends, I visited the local poolroom, Charlie's Billiard Academy on Boston Post Road, located right up the street from my home. I always had a good time there, socializing and playing pool with a lot of other guys. It was a lot better than hanging out in a bar and drinking, which I never approved of. Plus, I didn't drink. We played pool for only small amounts of money. Usually, I held my own in those games, never losing much, but never winning much either.

Most of the guys, who frequented the poolroom, were a little older than me because most of the younger guys had been drafted. Amongst the older guys, there was Tom, a cab driver; Joe Aiello, and his younger brother, Danny Aiello, (we called him Junior), who years later, would become a famous Hollywood actor; the Zani brothers, and Larry Goldberg. There also was a guy named Sal, who worked in Manhattan in the Garment District, from whom I was able to buy skirts and blouses for my sisters at very low prices. A couple of old timers, Lindy, and Stoney, were always there, they enjoyed putting on exhibition games for us. There was also Schmully, Honky, Frankie Laquato, and a guy named Jack, who used to be a boxer, but now he worked there taking care of the place.

On Saturday's, we usually played pool until late at night. Some of the girlfriends and wives of the players constantly called, telling them to come home. Sometimes they even went as far as, coming up to the poolroom and dragging them out of there. Once in awhile, after we played pool for most of the afternoon on Sundays, we piled into Tom's taxi, and went to Tremont Avenue to a very good Italian restaurant, and had dinner there. Other times we sent someone to Annie's Deli, to pick up some corned beef or pastrami sandwiches while the rest of us continued playing pool.

The poolroom, generally, has a bad reputation. In the movies, it's usually depicted as a hangout for crooks and gangsters, but that's not always the case. Yes, we had some bad characters hanging out there. They would burglarize houses, shoplift, and sell drugs, but we all stayed clear of them. At times some of the guys would go to the crap games, which were held on the roofs of apartment buildings and play. The police wouldn't bother anyone there. I went and watched, but I never joined in playing.

My mother was always very uncomfortable about me spending so much time in the poolroom, thinking that eventually, I would get into trouble. One day, when my brother, John, was visiting our mother, she asked him if he would go to the poolroom to find out what was going on there. I was in the middle of a pool game when John came in. He watched for a few minutes, and when he saw that I was winning some money, he asked me if we could go partners, which I thought was very funny. Then he went back to see our mother, and he reassured her that there was no need for her to be concerned.

Serving During the Korean War

After I had been in the National Guard for close to two years, I began to get lax and started to miss some of the meetings. I hadn't realized that by doing so made me eligible to be drafted. I was in shock and total disbelief, when I received my draft notice to report to Whitehall Street in New York City, to be inducted into the Army. In January of 1953, at the age of twenty-one, I was sent to Aberdeen Proving Ground in Maryland for eight weeks of basic training. It was the worst experience of my life. It was also the first time that, I had been away from home and my family for such an extended period of time. I missed my family, and I always worried about my mother. Your life wasn't your own. You got your crew cut and your Army clothes, then you were told when to eat, when to sleep, and when you could go to the bathroom.

We got up at five in the morning for roll call, braving the cold February wind coming in off the Atlantic Ocean, along with the rain and snow. A number of times, I was assigned extra duty, as being from the Bronx didn't set too well with most of the cadre, who were in charge of our barracks. Usually, they were from the southern states, and I think they were still trying to get even with the Yankees for winning the Civil War. There was a cadre, who went out of his way to harass me, and after a while, I decided the time had come to do something about it. Therefore, I challenged him to meet me behind our barracks after dinner, so I could have it out with him, but he never showed up. At the end of the week, I went to get my weekend pass, so I could come home, but I found it had been pulled. I went to see the Company Commander and asked him why my pass had been pulled. He explained that it was because I had challenged the cadre, which we had been told by our First Sergeant, you had the right to do if you thought that you were being unjustly harassed. Nevertheless, I lost the argument, but the cadre didn't harass me anymore after that.

Upon completion of the eight weeks of basic training in Maryland, I came home on a furlough for about a week. My mother worried about me being safe, so she gave me a scapular to wear just like the one, which she had given to Tony years earlier. Then I was shipped to Atlanta, Georgia, to attend wheel vehicle repair school. I spent twelve weeks there learning to be an auto mechanic, which I never really cared for. The smell of grease and oil never appealed to me. After all of us had completed our courses, we awaited our orders. The rumor was that everyone in my company was going to be sent to Korea. During the whole time, while I was in Atlanta and firmly believing in the power of prayer, I constantly prayed that I wouldn't be sent to Korea. I knew, I was incapable of killing another human being, and I didn't want to be put in that situation. While in Georgia, I was also able to earn my GED diploma.

Duty in England

When we finally received our orders, I was informed that I was being sent to England, along with another serviceman in my company, to be attached to the Air Force, the 928th Engineer Aviation Corps. We were told that everyone else in the company was being shipped to Korea. You can't imagine, how relieved and overjoyed I was, I couldn't wait to telephone my mother to tell her the news. I came home on leave for a few days. Then I flew to Scotland, and from there I boarded a train which brought me to the Army camp at Collier's End in England.

After arriving there, I reported to the personnel officer. I was fortunate, in that I had some previous experience working in a bakery, and I had earned a good grade as an auto mechanic. Therefore, I was given a choice of where I wanted to work. I could work in either the motor pool or take a position in the kitchen as a cook. Naturally, I chose being a cook where I would be working indoors and never be hungry.

The camp was a headquarters company with one hundred twenty-five personnel, along with a number of officers. I enjoyed cooking very much as well as being in England. Our camp was situated out in the countryside, surrounded by a number of quaint little towns. It was very pleasant and peaceful, so much different than living in the Bronx. We worked one day on and one day off, it was pretty good duty. There were a number of fellow servicemen, who were from the Bronx and Brooklyn, so we had a few things in common. Not far from our camp, there was a quaint little Catholic Church, which was several hundred years old where some of us would attend Sunday Mass.

Some of the other cooks and I often took a cab or bus to London on our days off. It was only about thirty-five miles from our camp. We visited all the major landmarks in London and enjoyed the famous English dish of fish and chips doused with a little vinegar wrapped in newspaper. Having been in England for about four months, I stopped by our NCO Club on Thanksgiving night after I had finished my shift in the kitchen. It was there, I met my future wife, Maureen, who lived in a neighboring town.

We dated for the duration of my tour in England, mostly on the weekends. She was seventeen at the time, five years younger than me. Maureen was nice looking with a terrific figure. I guess that I was infatuated with her. Maureen was also the first girl, whom I had ever gone out with. She lived in the town of Hoddesdon with her parents, and her younger siblings, a sister and a brother. There was a double-decker bus, which I took to Hoddesdon as it was about eight miles from my camp. We spent the evenings there, while her parents were out socializing at the local pub, or we went to see a movie at the local movie house.

When I left late at night, the double-decker buses only went halfway to my camp, leaving me off in a town called Ware. At that point, it was necessary to try hitching a ride back to camp. The town square was always deserted, and often it was very foggy at that time of night. I was usually the only one out there, and you could hear the echo of my footsteps walking down the street. There was a church steeple in the town square, where I saw bats flying in and out of it. It was a bit creepy, and I felt like I was playing a part in an English movie while waiting there trying to get a ride. Fortunately, I was able to hitch a ride back to camp most of the time. The few times when I didn't, I called the local taxi driver in town, and he drove me back to camp.

During my tour in England, I was able to get a furlough, along with a lift on a DC-7 Army Transport Aircraft to Nuremberg, Germany, where my brother, Tony, was stationed. I met his wife and son for the first time, spending a few days there. We did some sightseeing, and I enjoyed sampling the German sausages and their famous beer. We visited various landmarks including the Nuremberg stadium where Hitler held his massive rallies, and I stood on the podium where he gave his hypnotic speeches, before flying back to England.

While I was serving in the Army, my mother received my allotment, so it did help her with the finances. At one point, my mother wrote, telling me that my father had passed away. He had received an injury many years earlier, while at work, which eventually developed into terminal cancer in his neck and shoulder. My father was fifty eight years old when he died.

When I was first inducted into the Army, I was devastated about losing my independence and having to leave home. However, it was probably the best thing that ever happened to me. Serving in the Army made me more mature, and it really opened my eyes about the realities of life. While there, I met guys, who were better educated and already versed in some kind of trade or profession. It made me realize, that my life wasn't going anywhere. I knew that in order to improve my life, I would need to learn a trade or get a better education. I looked forward to the time, when I would be discharged from the Army, so that I could get on with my life. I was determined to make something of myself, so that I, too, would have a brighter future.

Returning Home

The Korean War ended, in July of 1953. I was still in the Army serving in England, until I was discharged in December of 1954, then I crossed the Atlantic Ocean for the second time on a ship. This time the trip to America on a military vessel was a lot more pleasant, and the Navy food was very good. Before leaving England, Maureen and I decided that we would get married after I returned home and was settled. I continued to correspond with her until the time came, when I could send for her to join me in America. While I was in the Army, Ronnie and our mother had moved into the Soundview Avenue City Projects in the Bronx. They moved to a building, which had an elevator since our mother had a heart condition, and she was no longer able to climb stairs.

After coming home, I lived with Ronnie and our mother in the projects. I visited some of my old haunts and found that, while I was away for close to two years, the Bronx had changed a great deal and sorry to say, not for the better. The drug culture had found its way into the neighborhood. By then, most of my single friends had been discharged from the service, and had married, and moved to either Long Island or New Jersey to safer neighborhoods.

I returned to my old job in the bakery, where I worked for a short time, while deciding, which trade school I should go to. Having served in the military, I was eligible to go to school under the G.I. Bill. It wasn't easy deciding whether I should go to a cooking school, which I enjoyed doing very much, or linotype school, as Richie had suggested. Linotype operators were earning a pretty good salary and the work wasn't difficult. (Linotype typesetting machines were the industry standard for setting the type for newspapers, magazines, and other materials, from the late 1800's to the 1980's. The linotype operator set the lines of type, prior to the copy going to the printing press.)

After spending some time, mulling it over, I decided that learning to be a linotype operator was probably the better choice. I then gave my notice at the bakery, and I enrolled in the linotype school, which was in Manhattan. It was a three-month course and during that time, I had to learn the keyboard, which was much different than a regular typewriter keyboard. I also had to learn the workings of the linotype machine. Learning the keyboard in the beginning was very difficult, but the longer I practiced, the easier it became. It wasn't physically strenuous because I was sitting down, but my eyes tired a bit after working for eight hours, until I got used to it. I do have to say, I have a lot to thank Richie for. He was very helpful in guiding me in the right direction, which enabled me to make the best decision.

Moving to Connecticut

By now, Richie was working for the Hartford Times Newspaper in Hartford, Connecticut, and he was earning a very good salary. He rented a small apartment in East Hampton, Connecticut and found that he liked the area. He drove back to New York for the weekends to be with his family. Eventually, Richie moved his family from the Bronx to join him in East Hampton. We were all eager to leave the Bronx, so after visiting Rose and Richie in East Hampton, all of us decided to try to find a two-family house there, so that we could all live together.

After searching for a while, Richie was able to find a vacant, two-family house for sale in East Hampton. Then Ronnie, our mother, and I went to look at the house. Once we visited the house, we decided that it was perfect for our needs, so Ronnie and I chipped in and put a down payment on it. The house was a fixer-upper and required quite a bit of work, but at that time, it was all we could afford to buy. After we purchased the house, we did some painting and repairs. Then Rose and Richie moved in first and lived on the second floor. Shortly after, Ronnie and our mother moved in and lived on the first floor.

I continued to live in the projects in the Bronx, for the duration of my schooling. It was shortly after everyone had moved to Connecticut, when I sent for Maureen. We were married in September of 1955. Maureen was able to get a job as a department store clerk in Manhattan, while I was still attending school.

Once I finished school, Maureen and I moved to Connecticut, and lived with Ronnie and our mother on the first floor of the house in East Hampton. We were happy to leave the projects in the Bronx because it was not a safe place to live anymore.

Our mother loved the house and was very happy living there. Finally, she had a place to call her own. She also had the constant company of Rose's three children, Kenny, Kevin, and little Jimmy, who was born shortly after, they relocated to East Hampton. The property had a large yard and a barn. Our mother was delighted, that now she was able to plant a large garden as she enjoyed growing her own vegetables. Later on, she even had a chicken coop in the barn and raised chickens. Every morning, our mother went out and gathered up the fresh eggs, which we enjoyed for our breakfast.

At one point, Richie decided that, he would plant his own garden. My mother and Richie competed to see, which one of them could grow the largest vegetables. My mother put some chicken manure into a bucket of water, let it ferment overnight, and the next morning, she used a ladle to douse the vegetables. Of course, my mother was the winner of the contest.

The three boys, Kenny, Kevin, and Jimmy, often came down to see what Grandma was making for dinner, when they didn't like what their mother was serving. At times, they would run to Grandma to escape Dad's anger. My mother always tried to calm Richie down, telling him that the boys were good kids. She had a calming effect on everyone.

Tony Comes Home from Germany

Tony had served eleven years, in Germany and came home to the United States in 1956, with his wife, Irmgard, and their nine year old son, Bernd. He rented an apartment in Yonkers, New York for his family, and he enrolled his son in the local grammar school. Meanwhile, Tony was stationed at Fort Dix in New Jersey. He came home on the weekends. Once Tony had finished his tour at Fort Dix, he was assigned to Kansas for a tour there. Before leaving for Kansas, he rented an apartment and moved his family to East Hampton, where they would have our help and company while he was away. Tony served in Kansas for three years, and occasionally he came home on a furlough.

My First Linotype Job

With Richie's help, I found a job as a linotype operator, set-ting type at a printing plant in New Haven. Maureen was able to find a job at a local bank in East Hampton, where she walked to work. I took a Greyhound bus to work, until Richie taught me how to drive, and then I bought my first car. It was a used car, but I was happy to have it as being able to drive myself to work was a nice convenience. While living in the Bronx, we all used the bus or subway system to commute. As most people didn't own cars, none of us had any reason to learn how to drive before. My sister, Ronnie, was able to find a job working in an office of a manufactur-ing plant in town. It was right down the street from our house, so she walked to work. Once Ronnie learned how to drive, she also bought a used car.

My wife, Maureen, had a very difficult time adjusting to our living arrangements. Moreover, she was homesick for England. After a while, we left East Hampton and moved into a furnished apartment in New Haven. Again with Richie's help, I was able to find an even better typesetting job at Southern New Eng-land Typographic Service, which was located in Hamden. My new job was very convenient as it was only a few miles from our apartment. I also earned more money, but unfortunately it was a night position. Being newly married and having to work nights wasn't an ideal lifestyle, however, at that time, I didn't have much choice.

I was able to gain a lot of experience in the trade working nights. Maureen found a job at a bank, which was right up the street from where we were living in New Haven. Sometimes dur-ing the day, while Maureen was still at work, I drove to East Hamp-ton and helped Richie with some of the improvements, which the house still needed. Maureen and I had been married, for about a year and a half, when we decided it was time to start a family.

Becoming a Father

On December 11th, 1957, our son, Stuart, was born. My plan was to have at least four children, so I thought that it was the beginning of a large family. I wanted our son to experience the same blessings that I had growing up with my sisters and brothers.

Shortly after Stuart was born, my wife informed me that she didn't want to have any more children, which made me very unhappy. I hoped that in time, she would change her mind, but she never did. My concern was, if anything should ever happen to my only son, then I would be left childless. After working nights for a couple of years, I was able to go on the day shift, which made our life more pleasant. We moved into a new apartment in Hamden and bought all new furnishings for it. Maureen was able to stay at home to raise Stuart. Luckily, my job was right down the street from where we lived, so I was able to walk to work. That enabled me to leave Maureen the car if she needed to go anywhere.

Ronnie Gets Married

My sister, Ronnie, worked in East Hampton for a while. However, now that she owned a car, she was able to look for a better-paying job. She applied for an office position at the Pratt & Whitney plant in Middletown and was hired. It was about ten miles from her home in East Hampton. It was there, she met Peter Laskarin, a widower with three children. Tragically, he had lost his pregnant wife, and their unborn child in an auto accident, due to a drunken driver. Pete and Ronnie enjoyed dating for several months, as they were happy and fell in love. Therefore, Pete asked her to marry him.

She was happy with his proposal, but she had a couple of serious reservations. Ronnie wasn't sure, if she wanted to take on the huge responsibility of having to raise his three children. She also realized that, should she accept his proposal, then our mother would be left living alone. Our mother was very happy for Ronnie and urged her to get married. She told Ronnie, not to worry about her, insisting she would be fine, and that everything would work out okay.

Our mother was always concerned, that if something should ever happen to her, then Ronnie would be alone. She was thrilled to see Ronnie getting married and having a life of her own. All of us were fond of Pete, and we felt that Ronnie had made the right decision. Pete adored our mother, and he greatly enjoyed her European cooking. Ronnie gave her notice at Pratt & Whitney, and they were married in 1961. Ronnie then moved to Middletown where Pete owned a house. She took care of the household, and she helped to raise Pete's three children; Pete Jr., who was seventeen, Chrissie, who was eight, and Joey, who was only two.

Tony Comes Home for Good

Once Tony had completed his three years in Kansas, his next assignment was to serve three years in South Korea. After completion of his tour in South Korea, he came back home to East Hampton and once again awaited his orders. Concerned, that he was going to be sent back to Germany, (which was a strong possibility) he asked John, who was still a member of the National Guard, if he would use his influence to have him assigned to the National Guard, as the Regular Army NCO. John helped him by arranging for an interview with, the Commanding Colonel of the 7th Regiment Armory on Park Avenue in New York City. After Tony was interviewed, he was granted the position. Fortunately, he would remain stateside for the remainder of his Army career. Tony and his family continued to live in East Hampton, where he would come home on the weekends, while he commuted during the week to New York City for his duties with the National Guard.

Chapter 7:

YEARS OF JOY AND SORROW

Living Alone

My mother was now living alone as Richie and Rose had moved into their new house, which they had built in the same town of East Hampton. Once they moved out, we were able to rent their second floor apartment to some tenants.

After a while, we decided that it would be best for our mother to sell the house as she was very lonely living there, and she was not in the best of health. Even though, all of us visited her frequently, we thought she would be better off taking turns living with my three sisters. My mother lived about three months, at a time, at each of my sisters' homes. My mother always felt as if she was imposing on everyone, even though, that was not true. Having to relocate from one home to another wasn't the best lifestyle for her health, and I think she was growing weary of the constant moving.

I felt very sorry for my mother as she didn't have a place of her own any longer. The only consolation I had was that, after living in apartments for a good part of her life in the Bronx, she had been able to enjoy living in her own home out in the country, and she had been very happy there for a number of years.

My Mother's Passing

Then on July 7th, 1964, while living with my sister, Ronnie, in Middletown, my mother passed away at the age of sixty-six. My wife telephoned me, while I was at work to say that Ronnie had telephoned and said my mother had died. I was in complete shock and dazed. I rushed home immediately and telephoned John and Tony, telling them the terrible news of our mother's passing. Of course they, too, were shocked and devastated.

What would we do without her? You always feel that the ones you love will be around forever. Sadly, that's not the case. I remember her asking me once, if I thought that when she died, would she go to Heaven? My reply to her was, the only way she wouldn't get to Heaven, was if there was no Heaven. Surely, God would welcome her into His Kingdom, after all her suffering and the many sacrifices she had made during her lifetime, along with the deep religious faith that she possessed and practiced.

I tried to compose myself, and then I drove to Ronnie's house. Everything seemed so unreal. When I arrived, Rose was already there. As I met them, we embraced one another and wept trying to console each other for our tremendous loss. After spending some time together, we went to the funeral home to pick out a casket for our mother. At that point, I still wasn't able to fully comprehend that our mother was no longer with us. A few days later, we were all in East Hampton at the funeral home attending our mother's wake, joining the local parish priest in prayers for her, and then taking turns to pay our respects at the casket. It was only when, it was my turn, as I knelt down and gazed upon her lying there, that I broke down and wept uncontrollably. Then, I realized that she was gone forever. I kissed her on the forehead and bid her a final earthly farewell, until I would see her again, which I know, I will.

The day she passed away, Ronnie said that our mother had been walking from the porch into the kitchen to get something, when she just uttered the word 'oh' and fell to the floor. Clearly, her weak heart had finally given out. I thanked God that she went suddenly and didn't suffer.

My Mother's Funeral

Something out of the ordinary occurred after my mother died, which made me feel that she was still close to me. On the morning of her funeral it was raining. I was sitting by a window in Tony's house in East Hampton, and outside on a tree near the house, there were a number of birds chirping. It seemed strange because it was raining very hard, yet there they were out there chirping away. My mother always loved listening to the birds singing. In a certain sense, it was as if, she was there with me listening to them. Shortly after, we all went to the Funeral Mass at St. Patrick's Church in East Hampton. Something unusual also happened at her burial. It was still raining very hard, but immediately after she was buried, the rain stopped, the clouds parted, the sun broke out, and it shone very brightly.

Later, after my mother had been buried in St. Patrick's Cemetery in East Hampton, I returned home, still feeling full of grief. Even though I was hungry, I couldn't eat as I had a sick feeling in the pit of my stomach. Instead, I lay down on my bed. I asked God, to "please take this pain away from me." Then within an instant, the pain in my stomach was gone, and I was fine. However, the overwhelming grief was still there. In the days that followed, I realized, my life would never be the same. With her passing away, a part of me died with her.

The one thing, which my mother had always longed for, was to go back to Czechoslovakia and visit our home in Trstany and to see her one surviving sister and four brothers again. Unfortunately, the doctor told her that, her heart would not tolerate the strain of the long trip. Therefore, she thought, if she couldn't go back there, then perhaps, she could have her favorite brother, Gustin, come to visit her in America. In the spring of 1964, my mother wrote to him and asked him, if he would like to visit her. He replied that, he would be thrilled to see her again. My mother sent him the funds for the trip to America. While he was making preparations for his journey, my mother passed away. We immediately notified Gustin of her death. He was deeply saddened, when he heard of her passing, and he decided to cancel his trip.

Throughout the years, we had always been a close-knit family, and even after our mother's death, we remained very close. We visited one another frequently, celebrated all the holidays together, had numerous cookouts, and went out to dinner quite often. Every year, on February 17th, we would go out to dinner to commemorate our arrival in America and reminisced about our journey here. Our mother was always foremost in our conversations. There's hardly a day, which goes by, that I don't think of her.

Going Into Business

As the months passed after my mother was gone, I felt more lost than ever. It seemed that my life wasn't making much sense anymore. I was working my full-time job, along with working part-time in the evenings and sometimes on the weekends to earn extra income, typesetting for printers. Hard as I tried, though, I never seemed to make any headway. Moreover, my marriage was falling apart. I was very unhappy and frustrated. It was then I sensed that, my mother was there by my side. Perhaps, it was because she knew of my sad situation and wanted to help me. I really can't explain it, but I had this strong feeling, she was encouraging me to take hold and to pursue my longstanding dream of going into business for myself, and that all would be well. What did I have to lose? Things couldn't be much worse, than they were now. Therefore, with a new resolve, I decided to take the plunge and start my own type-setting company.

The first thing, I did was to speak to the plant machinist, Max Benoit, about my plans. He thought it was a great idea, and he gave me a lot of information on how to get started. Max was a tremendous help to me. I thanked him for being such a good friend. Then I persuaded another friend of mine, whom I worked with, to go into business with me. This new venture was a gamble, but I felt, I had nothing to lose and everything to gain.

In November of 1964, we set up a corporation called Typographic Art. Both of us were equal partners. I didn't have any savings to speak of, but I was able to borrow six hundred dollars from my brother, John, to get the business going. My partner borrowed money from his father-in-law, for his share. We started the business on a shoestring, as we financed almost all of our equipment. Luckily, we were able to rent an over-sized two-car garage in Hamden very cheaply, and then we put a down payment on a rebuilt linotype machine, along with only the bare essentials of other equipment necessary to operate.

Our plan was to continue working at our current jobs, until we finished setting up our own shop. While we were in the process of doing that, one of our suppliers mentioned what we were doing to our employer, who upon hearing that immediately terminated both of us. Now we were on our own; forced to start the business prematurely. Once we had everything in place, we produced a type specimen book showing our few typefaces. Initially, we only called on printers, which generated some work for us.

After a while, we were able to add to our typeface library, and then we began calling on advertising agencies. We received our first big project through an advertising agency, which was to typeset the

Asgrow Seed Company catalog. During that time, we worked very long hours, six or seven days a week and many late nights. Eventually, after being in business for about six months, we started to do fairly well, and we were finally able to pay ourselves a small salary.

The First Anniversary

On the first anniversary of our mother's passing, my sister, Ronnie, had a strange experience. She was at home ironing clothes in the bedroom, which our mother used to sleep in, when she was living with Ronnie. Suddenly out of nowhere, she smelled the strong scent of lilacs and had the feeling of a presence in the room. Lilac was the same scent of the perfume, which our mother always wore. Ronnie was afraid that if she turned around, she would see our mother, so she didn't. Quickly, the scent of lilacs and the feeling of a presence were no longer there. Ronnie later regretted that, she hadn't turned around.

Single Again

After I had only been in business for a little over a year, my wife decided, that she no longer wanted to be married, so she filed for a divorce. At that point, I didn't have much choice, so I decided not to contest it. It had been a troublesome marriage, right from the very beginning, and I knew that things were never going to change.

As of April, 1966, after being married for almost eleven years, I was single again. It was very traumatic for me, no longer having a family and a home that I could return to at the end of the day. In a sense, I was homeless. Having to pay child support and alimony didn't leave me much money as I wasn't earning a decent salary yet. Frequently, I ate my meals at McDonald's as they were very economical. The only place, I found to rent was a room in a boarding house, where a number of other divorced fathers were also renting. After living there for a few years, I was able to afford to rent my own apartment, furnishing it with the bare necessities. Fortunately, I knew how to cook, so I was then able to eat my meals at home.

Still working six days a week and often late into the night, didn't leave me much time for any sort of a social life. I looked forward to Sundays, when I would pick up my son, Stuart. Often, we went to visit my sisters in East Hampton, and Stuart always had a good time there, while playing with his cousins. Whenever we went, our first stop was always the Jewish bakery in Hamden, where I bought all kinds of breads and pastries to bring with me to East Hampton. A second stop was McDonald's, to buy a hamburger for Ronnie's dog, Penny, an Irish-Setter.

Whenever, I arrived at Ronnie's house, Penny was already out there in the driveway, waiting to greet me. It was almost as if, she knew that I was coming. She was always so happy and overly excited to see me that, sometimes she would even piddle a bit while I was petting her. It was always the same scenario, as Penny was there with her tail wagging all over the place, waiting for me to give her the hamburger. As soon as I gave it to her, she held it in her mouth and raced off as fast as she could to bury it in the woods behind Ronnie's house. All the while, Ronnie's next-door neighbor's dog was sitting in her own yard, watching where Penny was burying her treat. The neighbor's dog waited, until Penny left, and then she dug it up and ate it. It was amusing to watch.

Stuart and I always stayed for dinner, and then I dropped him off at his mother's home in the evening. Other times, I spent the whole day with him, doing different things such as: taking him bowling, or fishing in the summertime, and often we would go the movies. It took awhile, for me to adjust to my new single life-style. In the beginning it was very difficult, but as time went on, it became much easier. I was fortunate in having my own business as it made things a lot more tolerable. Eventually, I began to enjoy my life again.

After a little more than a year, of working out of the garage, we moved the business to North Haven, where we were able to rent a storefront. Then we set up our office in the front portion, leaving ample room in the rear of the store, for the shop part of our business with our one linotype machine and other equipment. All of our hard work started to pay off, as our business was becoming more successful. Within a short time, we were able to afford to purchase additional linotypes, along with upgrading some of our older equipment. Moreover, my partner and I were able hire additional people, and finally we started earning a decent salary.

Bernd is Killed While Serving in the Vietnam War

While growing up in Germany, Tony's son, Bernd, felt proud of the fact that Tony was an American soldier. Tony and Bernd were buddies, spending as much time with each other as possible. Their world pretty much revolved around the Army.

Tony enrolled Bernd in the American school at the Army base in Germany as soon, as he was old enough to attend. Upon coming to America, he excelled in sports, especially soccer, which he had often played with his friends while growing up in Germany. During his high school years in East Hampton, he was a valued player on the soccer team. He was very popular and made friends easily.

In 1966, Bernd graduated from East Hampton High School. Tony then decided to move his family from East Hampton back to Yonkers, where the commute to his job in Manhattan would be much shorter. With the War still raging in South Vietnam, Bernd heard the call of duty and decided that he wanted to serve in the military, just like his father. More than anything else in the world, he wanted his father to be proud of him. Reluctantly, Tony gave his permission, and Bernd joined the elite fighting force, the 101st Airborne. After his basic training in Fort Benning, North Carolina, his outfit was shipped to South Vietnam.

Bernd had been serving in South Vietnam for a few months, and he had gone out on numerous patrols, both day and night. It was one day in the middle of the afternoon, during a patrol, when tragically Bernd was killed. He was shot in the back by a sniper, that he never saw, as he brought fire on a second sniper during the battle of Khe Sanh, on the 12th of March, 1968. It was his twenty-first birthday. With over six thousand American combat troops stationed in Khe Sanh, Bernd was one of the two hundred seventy-four, who lost their lives there.

Around the same time, while fast asleep in his home during the middle of the night, Tony woke up with a start, as Bernd's dog, Candy, a white German Spitz, was at the bedroom window, whining. Tony thought that was peculiar and was very concerned, thinking that, something dreadful might have happened to Bernd. After that, Tony wasn't able to sleep. The next day, with much apprehension, Tony reported for duty at the National Guard Armory. When he was in his office, Tony was informed by a fellow serviceman, that Bernd had been killed in action. His worst fear was realized, his only son was gone. How do you go home and tell your wife, that her son is dead? Shortly after, as is customary in the military service, Tony and his wife were formally notified by Bernd's Company Commander that Bernd had been killed instantly.

In what sadly, ended up being his last letter to his parents, Bernd wrote, "All I do now is dream of that day in December when I walk into our home and can say to you, 'Mom and Dad, I'm home.' Just think I'll be wearing a C.I.B. (Combat Infantry Badge) just like Dad had on his chest, and with that on my chest, along with my Wings, there's no one who can say that I haven't done my job for the great country we live in."

Bernd and I had corresponded a bit. While I knew that he was in extreme danger, I tried not to think about that. I just thought he would survive his tour of duty in South Vietnam, like his father had during World War II and then return safely back home. On hearing of his death, I was deeply saddened and regretted, I hadn't written to him more often.

Upon Bernd's death, there was a huge outpouring of support and sympathy. Both his wake and funeral were attended by family, friends of the family, dignitaries, dozens of military officers, fellow servicemen, a number of Bernd's friends, former classmates, and many townspeople. Tony and his wife, Irmgard, received numerous condolences, and some among them were from President Lyndon Johnson, Senator Robert Kennedy, Senator Javitz, and the Secretary of the Army.

Bernd's funeral service was held at the Congregational Church in East Hampton. Following the church service, Bernd was buried with full military honors in the Lakeview Cemetery in East Hampton, Connecticut.

Bernd was awarded the Bronze Star and the Purple Heart, just like his father, for his military service to his country, only his medals were awarded posthumously. On Bernd's gravestone is inscribed, "There's no one who can say that I haven't done my job for the great country we live in."

Sometime later, a 'Bell Tower' was built and dedicated at the East Hampton High School. The tower is in memory of the young men that were former students at East Hampton High School, who tragically lost their lives while serving during the Vietnam War. Bernd's name and the names of the other young servicemen, who perished are inscribed on the monument.

Going Home to Czechoslovakia

In June of 1969, five years after my mother passed away, I made the decision to go back to Czechoslovakia. My mother had never been able to go back there for a visit because of her heart condition, so I would be going in her place. It was something, which I had always wanted to do. Of course, Czechoslovakia was now a Communist country, and I felt a little uneasy about travelling there. When I told my family and several friends of mine, what I intended to do, they were all very apprehensive about my trip. It had only been one year, since the Soviets had invaded Czechoslovakia, but I didn't think there was any great danger in going there.

While planning my trip to Czechoslovakia, I decided to stop off and visit England first. I wanted to visit my old Army camp, even though, I knew it was no longer active. Therefore, I wrote to my former in-laws, letting them know that I was coming back to England for a visit. They invited me to stay with them. They said that, as far as they were concerned, even though Maureen and I were now divorced, they still considered me their son-in-law.

I packed two large suitcases, loaded with a variety of things including Levi Jeans, aspirin, and other medicinal items, which were very much needed in Czechoslovakia. Then I boarded a plane in New York. I arrived in England and spent a few days there, staying with Maureen's parents. While there, I did some sightseeing in London, visited my old Army camp, and then I flew to Prague.

Upon arriving at the airport in Prague, I was shocked to see the military officers patrolling armed with sub-machine guns. It was a little intimidating and made me feel a bit uneasy. I couldn't help, but notice, most of the people there were sullen and not at all friendly. That was understandable, though, as their country was once again being held hostage, this time by a Communist government backed by the Soviets, instead of the previous Nazi Regime.

I boarded a plane to fly to Bratislava, the capital of the Slovakian part of the country. Upon arriving in Bratislava, I spent the night in a hotel near the railway station and asked the hotel clerk to wake me up early the next morning, which he never did. Apparently, Americans weren't too popular there in those days. The reason being that, prior to the Soviet invasion of Czechoslovakia in 1968, the people there were led to believe that America would come to their aid and intervene with military force, should any foreign power threaten their country. Of course, America did not, just as they hadn't done in the Hungarian Revolution years earlier.

Fortunately, I used my battery alarm clock to wake myself up, and then I took a taxi to the train station, and I purchased a train ticket to the closest town near my village. As I tried to find my way to the proper track and struggled with my heavy luggage, a teenage Gypsy boy offered to help me carry one of my suitcases. I told him, that he needn't bother, but he insisted. I was a bit concerned, as to why he was so intent on helping me, thinking that perhaps, he was going to run off with it, and I wouldn't be able to pursue him. My thinking was such, because while I was growing up in Czechoslovakia, the Gypsies had a reputation of not being trustworthy as they generally tried to swindle people. Thankfully, I was wrong as he was very helpful. When I tried to reward him for his assistance, the boy refused to take any money. He was one of the friendliest persons that I met during my trip.

Meeting the Relatives

When I finally boarded the train, I wasn't sure if I was on the right one, so I asked some of my fellow passengers in Slovak to look at my train ticket. They reassured me, that I was on the right train, and I felt more at ease. As time passed, it seemed like I was on the train for an awful long time, so once again I asked the same question, and still I received the same answer. I just wanted to make sure, that I wouldn't end up in Russia. Finally, after many anxious hours on the train, I reached the town of Spisska Nova Ves, and then I boarded a bus for the last part of my journey to my village, Trstany.

As I sat on the bus my fellow passengers were curious, and they asked me where I was from and where was I going. I told them, I was an American, but that I was born in Trstany, and I had come back to visit my uncle, Gustin, and other relatives, and also to see my old home again. They were all very pleased to meet me and told me, that they knew Gustin. When the bus reached my destination, my uncle was waiting there to greet me.

I don't know what came over me, but when I saw him, I was overcome with a tremendous amount of emotion. I embraced him, broke down, and cried. The only thing that I can think of is, by returning there, I felt that I had fulfilled my mother's wish. He reminded me, so much of my mother. It had been thirty years, since I had last seen him.

My uncle was very happy to see me. My first night there, my aunt, Katrina, prepared a traditional Slovak meal for us. After we had finished the delicious dinner, and had a few drinks of home-made vodka, I told my uncle everything, which had happened since we left Czechoslovakia in 1939. I also reiterated some of what my brother, Tony, had told him years before. He was very happy to hear, that we were all doing well in America.

One thing, though, that hadn't changed and really brought me back to my early childhood days, was the fact, that they had no indoor plumbing. They still only had an outhouse, and water had to be fetched from an outside well. In the morning, we started the day with a small glass of 'Slivovica,' to get our blood flowing. It was probably very similar, to what moonshiners called 'White Lightning' in America.

I asked him, how they fared during World War II. Gustin said that the War didn't have a tremendous impact on them as their village was small, so the Germans didn't really bother with them.

They occupied the larger, more important towns, and cities. He did say, though, there were some men from other towns and villages, whom the Germans had inducted into their Army. Those unfortunate men were then sent to the Eastern front to fight the Russians. Sadly, they never returned home.

He told me, that toward the end of the War, the Russian Army came through the towns and villages chasing the Germans. The Russian soldiers would rape all the young and attractive women, they were able to find. Therefore, at the first sign of Russian troops coming, all of the young women fled into the woods and hid there, until the Russians left the area. However, the older men and women stayed behind. Then the older women tried to make themselves up to appear ugly and un-kempt, so that they weren't considered desirable. The young men also hid because the Russian troops would enlist them as laborers, if they were found. The Russians also confiscated whatever they wanted from the places that they occupied, saying that they were liberators and therefore, entitled to do as they pleased.

Gustin also mentioned that the school children had been forced to learn Russian, as the second language in Czechoslovakia during the Cold War. While traveling through the neighboring villages and towns, I saw the presence of a number of Russian troops and tanks. I wanted to take some pictures of them, but my uncle advised me not to, because he was afraid that it might create a problem for us, if I did.

Feeling at Home

Even though, I had left Czechoslovakia at a very young age, I felt as if, I had come home. Over the years, I often thought about my childhood and had reminisced frequently with my sisters and brothers about our many years, growing up there. Yes, even thirty years later, it still felt like home!

It was a wonderful feeling, to be able to reconnect with my relatives. While there, I relived some of my happy child-hood memories and enjoyed some of the Slovak dishes, which I hadn't eaten in years. One of the things, I enjoyed the most was being able to speak Slovak to everyone, as I hadn't done that since my mother had passed away. I was very happy to be back, but wished that my mother was still alive and there with me in Czechoslovakia.

I distributed the jeans, which I had brought with me to some of my cousins, who were all thrilled to get them, and I gave the can-dies and gum to the little ones. Several people, who were strangers came to me, and asked if, I had any American dollars that I would like to sell. I had to tell them, I didn't, as it was against the law to do that. I didn't want to jeopardize my standing there with the local authorities. However, I did bring a substantial amount of American dollars with me, which I gave out to some of my relatives. They in turn, sold them in exchange for the local currency and did very well. At that time, the American dollar was very much in demand everywhere.

I went to see the house in Trstany, where I was born and raised. Then I walked on the dirt road from my former home to the schoolhouse as I had done, so many times, before in my early years. The schoolhouse was still standing, but it was no longer used. I saw a little boy in my village, about seven years old, poorly dressed, and barefoot. It was as if, I was looking at myself some thirty years before. I also met with some of our former neighbors, who had helped us tremendously in the early years, when we had lived in Trstany.

Visiting Zdiar

After I spent several days with my uncle, Gustin, it was time to move on. I traveled to Zdiar, which was the town of my parents' birth, and it was also where most of my relatives still lived. When I arrived in Zdiar, all of my relatives were happy to see me. They were very surprised, that I still retained and spoke the Slovak language so well. I met all of my surviving aunts, uncles, and a number of my cousins.

One of my uncles, whom I met, was my father's younger brother, Stefan. He had led quite an adventurous life. He had been a hunting guide in Zdiar before the War and during the German occupation. As Uncle Stefan was fluent in German, he escorted the German officers when they wanted to go out and hunt in the nearby forests. They paid him very well, especially if they shot and killed some deer or wild boar. Once the Germans had been forced to retreat, and the Russians arrived at Zdiar, some townspeople, who resented my uncle for being friendly with the German officers, informed the Russians that he was a German collaborator. Upon hearing that, the Russians arrested him, and then they sent him to a prison labor camp in Siberia. After a few years there, Stefan bribed some of the Russian officers, and then he was able to return home. Stefan was known to have the gift of gab, and if anyone could talk himself out of a Siberian prison, it was he. Sadly, he died in his early seventies. The time that, he had spent in Siberia took a heavy toll on his health.

During my visit, I was asked by a number of my relatives, if things were better in America, or if I thought things were better in Czechoslovakia? I didn't have the heart to tell them the truth, so I simply answered them by saying, that things were pretty much the same in both countries. It was then, that I realized how ill-informed they were about America, to have asked me such a question. After being in Czechoslovakia for a while, I started to feel guilty knowing how much better off I was living in America, than they were living there.

Apparently, what the Communists tried to do was to paint a dismal picture of what life was like in America, so that the people would not envy us. In those days, people didn't have televisions there, only radios, which were controlled by the Communist government. That way, the government was able to keep the people in the dark about life in the free democratic countries.

Of course, things in Czechoslovakia had improved a bit, since we left there. They now had electricity and natural gas in their homes. Therefore, they didn't have to rely on wood for heat or to cook with, although, some people still used wood. There was now, even a bus service going from village to village. All in all, though, things hadn't changed that much in the thirty years, since we left. People there were still having difficulty making ends meet.

My Final Stop in Prague

In time, I said my goodbyes, boarded the train and headed for Prague, where my mother's sister, Agatha, still resided. Her husband had passed away, and she was now a widow living alone. I was amazed, when I met her and heard her speak. It seemed if I closed my eyes, it would have been, as if my mother was speaking to me. Aunt Agatha sounded so much like my beloved mother, that I felt an even greater affection for her.

When I visited downtown Prague with my cousin, Ladislav, we went to Wenceslas Square and viewed some of the damage, which the Soviets had inflicted on the city during their invasion a year ago. While there I couldn't help, but notice that all the buildings were covered in soot from all the coal they were burning. Everything seemed dark and gloomy. We visited the Old Town Square to view the famous Town Hall Clock. I was amazed at how deserted the square was. There were only a handful of people there and not many shops.

People were lined up in front of a few shops, trying to buy food. I didn't see any Russian troops or tanks there. Apparently, they were all stationed outside of the city. It seems that, the Communist system was great for the high officials in the government, who were in charge, while the rest of the country suffered in poverty. The standard joke amongst the people there was, "We make believe we're working, and the Communists make believe they're paying us."

I took a lot of home movies, while I was visiting Czechoslovakia. Upon my return home, I showed them to all my siblings. They were very pleased to be able to see the village and the house, which we were raised in. After they saw the movies, I told them that they, too, should go back there for a visit. My wish was for them to have the same enjoyable experience, which I had while visiting the old country.

For many years, I kept in touch with my aunts and uncles. I sent them some money and packages of clothes from time to time. Looking back now, I regret that I didn't do more to help them.

Ronnie's Sorrow

In 1971, Pete and Ronnie decided to sell their home in Middletown and build a larger one in East Hampton. Shortly after completing their new home, Pete was diagnosed with an advanced case of lung cancer. After a brief illness and a few surgeries, he passed away in 1972, at the age of fifty-three. After just eleven years of marriage, Ronnie was left alone to care for her two youngest step-children, Chrissie, age nineteen, and Joey, age thirteen. The eldest, Peter Jr., had since married.

Ronnie was frightened and insecure, as she now felt very uncertain of the future. I told her, "Don't be afraid, you can always rely on me, I'll do whatever, you ask of me. After all, you're my sister and my flesh and blood. You helped raise me, so of course, I'll be there for you, if ever and whenever, you need me." It was some-time later, when she told me that my commitment to her made all the difference in the world, to know she wasn't really alone, and that she had someone to count on if need be.

In time, Chrissie moved out and went on her own. When Joey came of age, he joined the Coast Guard. Both are now married. Ronnie continued to live in East Hampton for a while. Then she moved to Clinton, as she enjoyed being near the shore.

My Business Grows

Our move into the store front in North Haven worked out well. Eventually, we had a total of eight linotypes. A number of our new employees, who joined us, were from Southern New England Typographic Service, the same company that my partner and I had worked for, prior to starting our own company. We also hired two sales executives, who were able to generate a lot more business for us. Our business continued to expand. After six years, we were outgrowing our current location, and we felt, it was time to take the next step. While driving in Hamden, I noticed a building lot for sale in an industrial area. After viewing it with my partner, we decided to purchase it. Then we had a seven thousand square foot building built to our specifications, and we moved in by the fall of

1972. As we were watching our building being constructed, I had a great sense of satisfaction that I now owned a piece of property. I felt very good about that.

Tony's Passing

After Bernd's death, Tony started drinking heavily. He continued to serve in the military for close to thirty years, and then he decided to retire from the service at the rank of Sergeant Major. Upon his retirement, Tony joined the American Legion Chapter and the local VFW, which were in Yonkers. He spent his days, at both organizations playing cards and drinking. I was very involved in my business, so I didn't visit Tony very often while he was living in Yonkers, which I now regret. Tony felt a tremendous amount of guilt, as he blamed himself for his son's death because he had allowed Bernd to join the paratroopers, even though it had been against his better judgment. He tried to drown his guilt with alcohol. Sadly, after a few years of very heavy drinking, he became very ill and was diagnosed with cirrhosis of the liver in 1975.

Not long after, his wife, Irmgard, telephoned me, saying that I should come to their home in Yonkers to see my brother, as he was very sick and refused to get medical help. When I arrived, I was shocked to see the tremendous change in his appearance. His stomach was very swollen, he had lost a great deal of weight, and his face was drawn. I pleaded with him, to please let us take him to the hospital, so that he could receive treatment for his illness. He refused to listen to me or his wife, and all the while, he was still drinking. After a few days passed, Irmgard telephoned me again, to let me know that Tony was now extremely ill, to the point that he had agreed to go to the local VA Hospital.

From then on, he was in and out of the hospital as his illness was terminal. Members of the family and I continued to visit him, but we all felt helpless because there was nothing we could do for him. Prior to getting sick, he had been the picture of health, standing over six-feet tall, and weighing over two hundred and forty pounds. At the end, he was only skin and bones as the disease had slowly eaten away at him. It was heartbreaking to see.

He passed away, on January 22nd, 1976, surrounded by his family. On his deathbed, just moments before he died, he was staring at a blank wall and uttered the words, "yes, Mom, wait, I'm coming to you, yes, Mom, wait, I'm coming to you," in Slovak. Evidently, he must have seen our mother beckoning to him. He was just fifty-two years of age at his passing. I was always saddened, that he died such a tragic death and at such a young age.

Tony's wake and memorial service were held in Yonkers, New York. It was attended by his family, friends, and also a large number of his former National Guard servicemen from the Park Avenue National Guard Armory in Manhattan, the Yonkers VFW, and the American Legion Chapter of Yonkers. I returned home later that night, feeling terrible about his passing. I thought, perhaps, if I made myself a drink, I might feel better. I had a couple of drinks of vodka, but I found it only made me feel worse. Then I broke down and wept.

Several days later, Tony was buried with full military honors. As his funeral was private, only his family and closest friends were present. He had been cremated and his ashes were buried next to his son, Bernd, in the Lakeview Cemetery in East Hampton, Connecticut. On his gravestone is also inscribed, the insignia of the 2nd Ranger Battalion and the words June 6, 1944, Pointe Du Hoc.

A few days after Tony's funeral, my son, Stuart, was at our home in his bed sleeping, when he awoke and saw a figure in the corner of the bedroom looking at him. After blinking and rubbing his eyes, to make sure what he was seeing was real, he soon realized, it was my brother, Tony. Stuart said that Tony appeared for only a few seconds, but he looked healthy and young looking, probably in his thirties. I think Tony appeared to Stuart because they had always been close.

After Tony's death, I often played a song on a cassette tape, which was written and sung by John Denver called 'Looking for Space.' That song exemplified to me, how Tony must have felt about his life. Listening to it, always made me feel very sad.

One day, while driving my car and playing that song, a voice in my head said, "Don't grieve for him, he's here with me." The only thing I can think of was that, it was my mother telling me, Tony was okay, with her, and not to worry, or grieve for him any longer.

After Tony passed away, his wife, Irmgard, continued to frequent the VFW chapter in Yonkers. While there, she developed a relationship with a fellow member, who was a widower. I often telephoned offering to visit her, and telling her that if she needed help with anything, to let me know. However, she decided to distance herself from everyone in the family. She became very involved with her new friend, and eventually they ended up living together.

Chapter 8:

REALIZING THE AMERICAN DREAM

Land of Opportunity

As my business became increasingly more successful, it made me realize, just how fortunate I've been. I came to America with just the clothes on my back and had to persevere through some difficult times. However, even though, I didn't have much of an education, I was able to attain the American Dream. America is truly the land of opportunity. All it takes is a goal you want to achieve, determination, some luck, a lot of hard work, faith in God, and you can make your dreams come true.

Success in Business

Once we were settled into our own building, we purchased another six linotypes, which now gave us a total of fourteen. We also purchased other typesetting equipment. A number of new employees were hired as our business was rapidly expanding. We now had four sales executives, who were acquiring some impressive new accounts. One of our accounts was Stop and Shop. We did the typesetting for their weekly advertising circulars. Another account was Yale University, for whom we typeset and printed their diplomas, along with typesetting all of their journals and bulletins. Furthermore, we were doing work for numerous advertising agencies. Our sales executives were going to Hartford, Fairfield, Stamford, and New York City, calling on new accounts.

By 1975, the business was doing very well, and I was earning a very good salary. I no longer had to work those long hours, and I was able to take time off whenever, I wanted to. We employed over forty-five people, who were working three shifts around the clock to service our customers. Some of our other clients were Xerox, Vick Pharmaceuticals, and Western Publishing in New York City, for whom we typeset many books, including the popular Betty Crocker Cookbook. Moreover, we typeset the annual reports for General Electric, American European Bank, Exxon, Sunoco, Johnson & Johnson, and a number of other major corporations. Eventually, we typeset an average of twenty or more annual reports, for some of the most prestigious corporations in America, for a number of years.

I also purchased a high rise condominium unit in Hamden, just a few miles from my plant. I bought all new furnishings for the condo. My son, Stuart, who was now eighteen, decided to live with me. After my divorce, I wasn't in much of a hurry to re-marry. With my business now being very successful, I was pretty happy with my single life. I dated some, but I avoided having a serious relationship with anyone. On one Saturday night, I had a date with a particular woman, and when I arrived at her home, all five of her children were standing in a row waiting to greet me. That really scared me off!

In the summer of 1975, I decided to finance a trip to Czechoslovakia for Richie and Rose, so they, too, would have the same wonderful experience, which I had several years earlier. Ronnie accompanied them, and they had a great time visiting all of our relatives and our village. John and his wife, Mary, also visited there several times, throughout the years.

In 1978, I returned to Czechoslovakia, along with my sister, Ronnie. It had been nine years, since I was last there, and I was eager to return once more. First, we went to Prague and visited our aunt, Agatha, for a few days. Then, we continued on to our village, Trstany.

While there, we stayed with our uncle, Gustin, for a while, before traveling to Zdiar to visit the rest of our relatives. After spending three weeks there, we returned home to the United States.

Photo Typesetting Technology

As the years rolled by, a new form of typesetting technology came into being, which was photo typesetting. By 1980, most of our competitors had installed the new system, and we, too, were forced to purchase that system to be able to compete. For a while, we operated with both hot metal and photo typesetting. We hired a few people, who were experienced in photo typesetting, and our sales executives were now able to service our customers with that system as well. After doing a cost effective study of both systems, we realized, that photo typesetting was far more efficient and had a much higher profit margin than hot metal. Therefore, we slowly made the transition of going completely from hot metal to photo typesetting.

Eventually, we sold all of our hot metal equipment, except for the very first linotype, which we had started our business with. We kept it as our good luck charm. Unfortunately, we had to lay off most of the hot metal employees as they had a difficult time adapting to the new system. We replaced all our linotypes with state-of-the-art computers and keyboards. As new employees were hired, they were sent to school for training on our new system. Before long, our plant was operating efficiently. With the new system, we retained our client base and acquired additional new business as well. All three shifts were in full operation. Business was booming!

Big Changes for Richie

Meanwhile, Richie wasn't feeling well, so he went to see his doctor. After being examined and having some tests, the results were unsettling. Richie's doctor informed him, that he needed to undergo a heart bypass operation. After the operation, he was in a coma for ten days. We were all deeply worried and praying for him, to come out of the coma and for his condition to improve. Thankfully, he recovered and after a recuperation period, he was fine.

Once he was well enough, he returned to work at the Hartford Times Newspaper. Unfortunately, soon after returning to work, the newspaper plant closed. Richie was now unemployed. As he was in his fifties, he found it very difficult to find another job. In 1980, I gave Richie a position in my company as a proofreader, along with various other duties. He sold his house in East Hampton and bought a house in North Haven, where the commute to work was much shorter.

Living the American Dream

My business pretty much allowed me to live the 'American Dream.' I was able to do a lot of traveling, drive nice cars, dine in fine restaurants, and share some of the fruits of my endeavors with my son and family. My only regret being, that my mother didn't live long enough to see it all happen and to share in it, there was so much, I wanted to do for her.

My business success afforded me the opportunity to possess something, that I always wanted, which was to own a house. Having lived in my condo for six years, I started to look for a building lot, where I would be able to build the house of my dreams. After exploring some areas, I found a building lot in Hamden. It had a magnificent view, I could see for miles and miles in every direction. Immediately, and without any hesitation I purchased it. Then I hired an architect and a building contractor. The three of us worked together, with the house being designed and built to my specifications. The condo, which I had previously lived in, was sold in 1981. Then I moved into my new contemporary style house. I also bought new furnishings. I had accomplished my last goal, finally having a home of my own! I thought it was a great house, and my son and I enjoyed living there.

By 1984, my son, Stuart, decided he wanted to be on his own, so I purchased a condominium in Hamden, not far from my house for him to live in. I was now living alone once again.

D-Day Anniversary

In June of 1984, the 40th Anniversary of D-Day, President Reagan and his wife toured the beaches of Normandy in France. They also met with the surviving veterans of the 2nd Ranger Battalion, who succeeded in the bloody assault on Pointe Du Hoc. They were all assembled at the site of the Dagger Memorial Monument, situated at the top of a cliff. The President and his wife were shown on television, standing and gazing at the high cliffs and at the beaches below, where forty years before on the early morning of June 6th, 1944, the Rangers had landed. All of the major networks televised it. I remember watching it and feeling sad and disappointed that my brother, Tony, wasn't still alive. It would have been wonderful if he, too, could have been there, alongside his surviving fellow comrades, on that momentous occasion. After watching the ceremony, I decided that someday, I would go to Normandy and see it for myself, to try to envision, what it must have been like to have been there on that terrible day.

Sharing My Good Fortune

By 1986, my company was earning revenues of over three million dollars a year, employing more than sixty employees, and I was earning a six figure salary. With my earnings, I was able to help some members of my family, financially. I sponsored trips for Ronnie, Rose, and Richie to Hawaii and on a Caribbean cruise. I purchased an ocean front condominium in a high rise building in Boca Raton, Florida, which was there for me and my family members to use and enjoy on vacations.

Throughout the years, there were numerous cookouts at my home. All of my family and friends were there, and everyone had a great time being together. Often on the weekends, I took everyone in my family out to dinner. I also chauffeured Richie, Rose, and Ronnie to New York City, a number of times, to enjoy the sights and dine at various restaurants. We particularly enjoyed eating at Katz's Deli. From time to time, I visited some of my friends that I had grown up with in the Bronx, and I took them out to dinner as well. We enjoyed reminiscing about old times.

My belief being, that as I had been blessed with success, I felt that, it was my obligation to share my good fortune with my family and friends. Making people happy is something, I enjoy doing. I know if my mother were still alive, that's what she would have wanted me to do.

John's Retirement

As the years went by, John was promoted numerous times, while at Lederly from working in the cafeteria, to working in the kitchen cooking, and helping with the food preparations. After years of hard work, he received the appointment to be the head chef. Eventually, he became the food service manager, catering to more than eighteen hundred employees daily. In January of 1986, after working more than thirty years at Lederly, John decided to retire. Being that John came from humble beginnings, and didn't even have a high school education, and was self taught, I'd say, he accomplished a great deal during his lifetime.

Upon his retirement, the company arranged a retirement party for him. John's wife, Mary, and their four children, along with Ronnie, Rose, and I were present at the party. Some four hundred fellow employees attended, bidding John farewell including Lederly's Chief Executive Officer and a number of Corporate Officers. It was the largest turnout, ever in the company's history, for a retiring employee. As a special tribute to John, they named the newly constructed cafeteria 'JB's' after him.

They asked him, what he planned to do upon retiring. John told them, that he wanted to go back to the South Pacific and visit the various islands, which he had served on while fighting the Japanese forces during the War. Once they were aware of that, they offered to pay for his entire trip. Before making any arrangements for his journey, John consulted with his physician. Much to his disappointment, the physician advised him, not to go. It would be very risky for him because John had been infected with malaria a number of times. At his advanced age, if he were to get infected again, it might prove to be fatal.

When John informed Lederly, that he was forced to cancel his plans because of the health risks involved, they presented him with a gift of five thousand dollars instead. He was only able to travel as far as Hawaii, due to his health, where he toured the War monuments. He was in his eighties, when the Army finally sent John his long awaited medals, including the Bronze Star for serving his country in the South Pacific. We're very proud as members of our family had been awarded three Bronze Stars and two Purple Hearts. Two of John's sons, Johnny, and Michael, also served in the Armed Forces.

Visiting the White House

While Ronald Reagan was President, my company typeset special programs for the White House through an advertising agency in Westport, Connecticut. For five years, we typeset the Annual Easter Egg Hunt and the Fourth of July Celebration brochures. We always received a credit line, along with other large prestigious corporations in the brochures. I felt very proud and happy to see that. Out of all the typesetting companies in America, my company had the honor of donating its services to the White House.

I thought back about my humble beginnings and the great difficulties I had endured, yet here I was doing work for the White House. I received special thanks from the White House for my company's contributions, for the special events, which they held. In addition, I received a Christmas card from President Reagan.

Then in the spring of 1986, Ronnie, John, his wife, Mary, and I went to Washington D.C. As I had previously, donated my company's typesetting services to the White House, I was able to arrange for a special private tour of the White House. While standing in the Rose Garden, I thought of my mother. Who would have ever thought, during those early years in Czechoslovakia, that we would now be standing in the Rose Garden at the White House! I think my mother would have been very pleased and proud to see that.

While visiting our nation's capital, we did a lot of sight-seeing and visited the various historic monuments of major importance. High on our list of priorities was the Vietnam Veterans Memorial, where Bernd's name was engraved on the Wall, along with some fifty-eight thousand names of those, who gave their lives in the Vietnam War.

The Centennial Celebration

Having contributed to The Statue of Liberty-Ellis Island Centennial Commission in 1985, my name is recorded on the Register of Contributors at the museum of the rebuilt Statue of Liberty. Therefore, in 1986, Ronnie and I went to Battery Park in New York City, to join in the July 4th Centennial Celebration of the Statue of Liberty. The Statue was unveiled and illuminated by President Reagan for the first time, since it had undergone restoration. Then Neil Diamond sang a rousing rendition of 'Coming to America.' It was very moving and sent chills up and down our spines, as we remembered our arrival in the New York City harbor, some forty-seven years before, huddled together on the ship's deck with the other immigrants on that cold winter morning in February, 1939.

Being there, brought back some sad and bitter memories of what my family and I went through in those early days, so long ago, how far we have come, and all that we have achieved. When we arrived by ship in the New York City harbor, I think we perfectly fit the criteria of what the Statue of Liberty symbolizes, with the words 'Give me your tired, your poor, your huddled masses...' The celebration continued with more inspirational music and a thirty-minute display of spectacular fireworks. Overall, it was a beautiful and thrilling experience. I will always treasure, being there on that momentous occasion, along with the thousands of others, who joined in the celebration.

Meeting Mona

It was in December of 1986, when I met Mona. She was a sales representative for a limousine service and called on my company. She was very attractive with a nice figure. Both of us, it seems, had an instant attraction to each other. She also was divorced and didn't have any children. Mona is blessed with a great disposition, a wonderful sense of humor, is extremely bright, and very honest. Moreover, she has a great deal of common sense and loves to do for others. Our first dinner date was on her thirty-second birthday. Even though, she is much younger than me, we have a lot in common and greatly enjoy each other's company. In the following years, we traveled extensively throughout the United States, Canada, Europe, and went on a few cruises. I was happy when one day, Mona told me, that I made all of her travel dreams come true.

It was only, by being with Mona that, I became more involved in doing charitable things for others, especially people, whom we don't know personally. Her genuine concern for others, made me realize, just how much joy there is in giving. Mona particularly, enjoyed donating toys at Christmastime to various children's hospitals and the Salvation Army. She received some monetary contributions from personal friends, along with our contribution, and then she purchased toys throughout the year. There were several years, when she donated more than one hundred toys. Mona has been involved in a number of charities, and she also has done fund raising for various organizations. Her main areas of concern have always been children, the elderly, and the poor. Mona and I continue to be involved in various ways. One area we focus on, is in doing for the homeless in our area, such as making sandwiches and donating clothing, along with other needed items.

Irmgard's Passing

In March of 1988, Irmgard passed away after a brief illness. My son, Stuart, and I, along with other family members, attended her wake and memorial service in Yonkers, New York. Irmgard was cremated and her ashes were buried, alongside her husband, Tony, and their son, Bernd, in East Hampton, Connecticut.

Upon her death, my brother, John, was able to obtain some of her personal items from her live-in companion, which only consisted of some photographs and papers, a few of Tony and Bernd's minor medals, along with some of Bernd's personal letters from the time, when he had been serving in South Vietnam. Everything else was gone, including the American military funeral flags, which had been awarded to Irmgard, for the loss of both her husband and her son, along with their Bronze and Purple Heart Medals.

A short time later, John gave me what was left of Tony's things, which he had put in a small valise. After going through the valise, I stored it in my basement. As the years went by, from time to time, I would look at the valise and feel terrible. I realized that, the only things left from Tony's life, were now in that little valise. It was then

I knew that, at some point, I would have to do something, so that his story would be told and not forgotten.

Midnight Visitor

One Saturday night, in the summer of 1988, Mona spent the night at my home. She slept in the guest bedroom, and I slept in my bedroom. Both bedrooms were on the second floor and across the hall from each other. Suddenly, I awoke from a sound sleep and saw a dark figure standing at the foot of my bed. I wasn't startled or frightened at all. I just stared at the figure for a few seconds, not being able to distinguish whether or not, it was Mona. Nothing was said. Being very sleepy, I assumed it was Mona, so I just turned over and went right back to sleep.

During our breakfast the next morning, Mona said, she had woken up during the night with the feeling of being watched. It was then, that she saw a dark figure standing at the bottom side of her bed, when suddenly the figure appeared by the bedroom window, and then it was standing in full view by the bedroom door on the other side of the room. The figure was dark, not tall, and the outline seemed to be that of a woman, but she could not make out the face. Mona remembered being awake and sitting up looking at the dark figure by the bedroom door.

She said that, she was not frightened, as it just seemed like the being had a right to be there. Therefore, she just lay down and went right back to sleep. Mona said, she was not able to explain why, she wasn't at all frightened. I was taken aback by what she said. Then I told her that I, too, had seen a dark figure at the foot of my bed in the night, but I assumed that it was her. However, Mona said, she had not come into my room during the night. It was such a strange happening, the two of us seeing the same figure on the same night.

To this day, I'm still puzzled about that night. We both woke up out of a sound sleep, saw a figure standing in each of our separate bedrooms, and we weren't frightened at all. Normally, if you were to experience something like that, you would be startled or afraid, and turn on the light, or jump out of bed. However, we didn't do anything except go right back to sleep. Evidently, whoever or whatever it was, didn't intend to do us any harm.

We both agreed, the figure was a female, but we could not make out any other features because it was dark. Mona thinks that the figure was my mother. I had a security system in my home with motion detectors on the ground floor, which was on that night, as it was every night. Therefore, no one could have entered my home, without setting off the security alarm. In addition, all the windows in our bedrooms, on the second floor, were shut and locked. The only thing, I can think of is that, it had to be a heavenly entity paying us a visit.

Chapter 9:

THE LATER YEARS

A Free Czechoslovakia

In October of 1990, Mona and I traveled to Europe. Our first stop was the city of Prague in Czechoslovakia, to visit my aunt, Agatha, whom I hadn't seen since my last visit in 1978. She was now in her late eighties and blind, but otherwise in good health. Agatha lived with her son, Miroslav, his wife, Hana, and their daughter, Hana, in a small apartment. Their apartment was in one of the austere concrete high-rise apartment projects, which the Communist government built all over certain parts of Prague and in other areas of the country as well. The buildings were constructed from pre-fabricated and pre-stressed concrete, called 'panel housing.' Prague was basically the same as it had been on my previous visit.

After checking into the Palace Hotel and spending some time with my aunt, Agatha, and her family, we decided to tour Prague. Therefore, we hired two college students, who also worked part time for the hotel as tourist guides. While touring the city, both young men were pleased when we asked them about the 'Velvet Revolution.' They told us with great pride, about the time of the mass rallies in Wenceslas Square. They went on to relate, how a large number of students brimming with hope and enthusiasm, went out into the city and knocked on doors, encouraging the people within to join in the demonstrations. All the people knew that this was their best opportunity, once and for all, to oust the current Communist government leaders and regain their freedom.

The Czechs succeeded in causing the downfall of the Communist regime. A free Democratic government was brought forth by the Velvet Revolution in December of 1989. It had only been ten months, since regaining their freedom, but already positive changes were happening. The future looked bright as Czechoslovakia was finally free!

It was wonderful to have visited a free Czechoslovakia, knowing now that the people's lives were going to continue to improve, after having been oppressed for so many years. Once we left Czechoslovakia, we continued on to visit Austria and Switzerland, and then we returned back home to the United States.

The Immigrant Wall of Honor

In 1992, Mona and I visited the newly restored Ellis Island and its on-site museum. My contribution to The Statue of Liberty-Ellis Island Foundation Fund, along with the fact that our family had immigrated to America, allowed our name to be registered and engraved on 'The American Immigrant Wall of Honor' situated on Ellis Island. It is engraved as 'The Anton Bachleda Family came to the United States of America from Czechoslovakia.'

Relocations

Throughout the years, members of my family relocated to different parts of the country. Many years earlier, Mary and Al had moved from New Jersey to Hendersonville, North Carolina. Several years later, my sister, Ronnie, left Connecticut and joined them there. Now retired, Richie underwent a second heart bypass operation, and thankfully, this time there with no complications. Once he recuperated, Rose and Richie relocated to Boynton Beach, Florida where they purchased a condominium. Having spent some time, living in our condo in Boca Raton, Stuart decided to live there permanently. Therefore, I sold the condo in Hamden, which Stuart had been living in, prior to moving to Florida. After living in Boca Raton for a while, Stuart married his girlfriend, Lynette, and they moved to a house in Deerfield Beach. Then I sold the Boca Raton condo.

Forced Retirement

My partner and I had been in the typesetting business for close to thirty years. At one time, we employed six sales executives and more than sixty employees working three shifts. However, the advent of the computer age pretty much forced us out of business. More and more people were doing their own typesetting on their computers. I was in a dilemma. What should I do? I didn't think that retirement was an option, and I felt an obligation to our employees. Several of them were close friends, who had been with us from the beginning. I was torn between venturing into the printing business, which my partner was in favor of doing, or investing in a fast food franchise, which I had always thought about doing, as I always enjoyed cooking for and feeding people.

In early 1993, after much deliberation, indecision, and the constant pressure from my partner to pursue the printing trade, I agreed to go into the printing business, even though I had serious reservations about it. It turned out, to be the worst decision I ever made. I should have listened to my gut feeling and also taken Mona's advice, not to pursue such an enormous new business venture. During that time, I was stricken with a serious case of pneumonia, and I was bedridden for about three weeks. Mona took care of me, until I got better. Once I recovered, I persuaded her to move in and live with me. After only a year and a half, in the printing business, things were looking very bleak. With the recession now in full swing, fierce competition, lack of work, the low profit margin in printing, and going deep into debt, trying to maintain it, we were forced to liquidate the business. We closed the plant in June of 1994.

The venture into the printing business was very costly, and it taught me a valuable lesson. Never invest in a business, that you don't have any experience in. Make sure, you know exactly what is involved. I knew every aspect of the typesetting business from selling it, to producing it, and finally billing it. I knew absolutely nothing about the printing business, and I had to rely on other people for advice, which is not a good business practice. It had been necessary for me to sell my home at a tremendous loss, due to a poor housing market, which had been caused by the recession. Along with some other disastrous real estate investments, a great amount of my savings was gone. Now at the age of sixty-three, I was forced to go into early retirement. I had limited financial capital left to venture into any new business, and I couldn't risk any of the few assets, which I still had left.

In 1995, after I sold my home in Hamden, Mona and I rented a condominium in Monroe, Connecticut. I was very depressed and insecure at times. I felt that, my whole world had crumbled into bits and pieces. I had been involved in my own business for thirty years, and I had earned a very good income from it. Now unemployed, with nothing to do, was very difficult for me. It seemed that everything, I had worked for all those years, was almost gone. The future looked very dim.

During that difficult time, I was thankful for all the help, understanding, and encouragement that Mona gave me. I don't know how, I could have survived without her constant support. She was at my side, through thick and thin.

It was then, that the strangest things began to happen. While I was sitting on the couch, during the day watching television with the windows open, all of a sudden out of nowhere, I smelled the strong scent of lilacs. My thought being, there must be some lilac bushes nearby. Therefore, I looked outside to see if there were any, but there were none. From that day onward, I often smelled the scent of lilacs, especially when I was feeling very depressed. Then I remembered that, lilacs were my mother's favorite flower. It was also the perfume scent, which she always wore. That was the same scent, Ronnie had experienced years before, when she felt our mother's presence in her home. I believe that, it was my mother trying to reassure me, that everything would be alright, not to worry, and that she was still there with me.

Remembering Tony

While living in Monroe, I read an article in a local newspaper, The New Haven Register. It was about a Ranger, who was involved in the assault on Omaha Beach, during the Normandy invasion on D-Day. I called the reporter of that article and told him about Tony and his son, Bernd. The reporter met with me, and once the interview was over, he said that, he thought it was a very interesting story. Therefore, he agreed to write an article.

The article later, appeared in the New Haven Register on Veteran's Day, November 11th, 1995, and was entitled 'Glory and Tragedy of War Become a Family's Legacy.' The article told the story of Tony being in the Rangers, and about him being wounded, and taken prisoner at Pointe Du Hoc on D-Day. The article also told of Bernd's desire to emulate his father. However, in so doing, Bernd lost his life while serving in Vietnam. After reading the article, I was satisfied that people would now know of the sacrifices, which

Tony and his son had made for their country. I had finally fulfilled the promise that I had made years ago, and I felt much better about having done so.

Moving and Getting Married

In June, 1996, Mona and I decided to move to Florida. I purchased a condominium in Boynton Beach, very near to where Rose and Richie lived. My son, Stuart, and his wife, Lynette, were now blessed with two children, a daughter, Sharyn, and a son, Austin. We were just a few towns away from where Stuart and his family lived in Deerfield Beach, which enabled us to visit them fairly often. Ronnie had remarried and still lived in North Carolina. Fortunately, she and her husband also had a second home in Florida. We enjoyed a lot of family gatherings while we all lived in Florida.

Mona and I had been together for ten and a half years. We loved each other and wanted to spend the rest of our lives together. Happily, on May 10th, 1997, we were married in Boynton Beach, Florida. We had an intimate church ceremony and a reception afterwards. After having lived in Florida for one and a half years, both of us decided that, we didn't want to make it our permanent home. The lifestyle there was not to our liking. It was extremely hot and humid in the summertime. Traffic was very congested and there were many car accidents. We never felt safe as the crime rate was very high in Florida. We missed seeing our friends, the seasons, and the New England lifestyle. Therefore, in April of 1998, we moved back to Connecticut and rented an apartment in Hamden for several months. Then we found and purchased a townhouse condominium in North Haven, where we still reside. Several years later, Stuart and his family relocated to Tennessee. Occasionally, I visit them, and sometimes they come to Connecticut and visit us.

Operation Christmas Child

While living in Florida, we learned about Samaritan's Purse. It's a charitable national and international relief organization. The head of the organization is Franklin Graham, son of the well-known preacher and public speaker Billy Graham. Samaritan's Purse provides relief and support for people all over the world in times of war, natural disasters, famine, disease, and poverty. There are several programs, which they offer, anything from buying a goat for a family to be able to sustain themselves to a marital counseling retreat in Alaska for war veterans and their spouses.

Our favorite program is the one called Operation Christmas Child. It is unique in that it is simple, and doesn't have to cost a lot, yet to its recipients, it is so much more. It's also very enjoyable to do. Anyone can do it: individuals, families, religious organizations, and civic groups. It consists of filling a shoe box for a child with various items such as: coloring books, crayons, school supplies, toys, little cars, dolls, stuffed animals, soap, toothbrushes, toothpaste, combs, t-shirts, socks, hard candy, and gum. Then it is marked, whether it is for a girl or boy and for the appropriate age group, two to four, five to nine, or ten to fourteen. The boxes are then shipped all over the world, mostly to third world nations for children suffering from poverty, disease, and either, natural or manmade disasters. They are shipped and distributed at Christmastime, and often the distribution carries over into the following months.

When I saw the shoe boxes and what Mona had filled them with, I thought it was wonderful. Having grown up very poor myself, I never had any toys or received any Christmas presents. Therefore, I could really identify with the program. I told Mona, how thrilled and overjoyed that I would have been as a child while living in Czechoslovakia, if I had received a shoe box filled with some of those cherished items.

It is still one of our favorite charities, and we continue to donate to the program each year.

Visiting the Czech Republic and Slovakia

On January 1st, 1993, Czechoslovakia was mutually divided into two completely independent countries. The western portion was now the Czech Republic, and the eastern portion was Slovakia. In 2000, my wife, Mona, and I again visited Prague in the Czech Republic, and then we visited Slovakia, which Mona had never been to before.

We flew to Prague and arrived at an impressive new airport. Prague was very different from our last visit in 1990. What a difference ten years can make! It seemed that after years, of being in a deep slumber it had finally awakened as the oppressive veil of Communism, which covered the city, had been lifted. Now the city of Prague, referred to as the city of one hundred spires, was being restored to its former magnificence. Many of the beautifully detailed architectural buildings had been cleaned and painted, while other buildings were still in the process of being redone. Specialty shops and department stores were located throughout the city, and there were many new restaurants, known for their culinary excellence. Tourists filled the squares and streets. It was such an amazing transformation. The city was alive again!

We arrived at the Palace Hotel and noticed that now the hotel staff spoke several different languages besides Czech, mostly German and thankfully for us, English. The atmosphere was very different, than our last stay at this same hotel. People filled the lobby and the staff was energetic and smiling. After we settled into our room, we took a cab to visit my cousin Miroslav's wife, Hana, and her family. Fortunately for Mona, Hana knew some English. Sadly, my aunt, Agatha, and her son, Miroslav, had both previously passed away.

In the following days, Mona and I did a lot of walking and sightseeing. We visited all the major sites, such as Wenceslas Square, Prague Castle, St. Vitus's Cathedral and its Chapel of St. Wenceslas. Another stop was the Church of Our Lady Victorious with the original statue of the Holy Infant of Prague. We also saw the Charles Bridge with it multitude of statues, and of course, the statue in the square of Charles IV. Then we visited the Old Town Square and its famous Town Hall Clock, with its moving procession of the Apostles and other figures.

Then it was time, to continue on to Slovakia. We took a very long train ride to the city of Poprad. My cousins, Jan, and Stefan Oleksak, met us at the train station and drove us to the Grand Hotel in Stary Smokovic. It was a beautiful hotel, set high up in the Tatra Mountains. We visited all my relatives in Poprad, including my father's sister, Rose, and my mother's brother, Valent. They were both in their nineties and still in fairly good health. One day, we spent time exploring the mountains with my cousin, Stefan, and another day, we visited one of the amazing caverns in the area with my other cousin, Jan.

A few days later, my cousin, Jan, drove us to Zdiar to visit the house, which my mother was born and raised in. It was still in very good condition, and Jan rents it out to tourists. Then we went to see the beautiful and picturesque church in town and attended Sunday Mass there. Later on, we visited with some other relatives. Mona loved Zdiar, as it is a small town with houses, surrounded by fields of farmland and the majestic High Tatra Mountains. She also enjoyed the fresh mountain air and all the farm animals.

Then we went to the small village of Hincovce, and visited with more of my relatives. Next we went to the nearby village of

Trstany, where I was born and raised. While there, I showed Mona the house where I was born, but we weren't able to go inside. The barns were still standing, and it looked much the same as when I had lived there. We visited the church and saw the schoolhouse, which I had attended. A highlight of the trip was our visit to Spis Castle, the largest one in Slovakia. Tony and his friends used to explore the tunnels underneath the castle and search for treasure, which was rumored to have been hidden there. We also saw a large Gypsy compound in the area. It was made up of shacks, where they lived in poor conditions. It was very sad to see.

While in Slovakia, even though, hardly anyone spoke English, we did see a lot of changes, since the fall of Communism. Poprad even had a McDonald's and a Pizza Hut restaurant. Many more new houses were being built in the various towns and villages. Everyone now had televisions with satellite dishes and VCR's. Most of the houses had modern plumbing with running water, bathtubs, showers, and flush toilets. Children had all sorts of toys, including bicycles. In general, people were happier now and much better off than they used to be. We didn't want to endure the long train ride back to Prague, so we flew there from the city of Kosice instead. Upon arriving in Prague, we spent a few additional days there, before flying back home to the United States.

Woman at the Grave

Throughout the years, Mona and I visited Bernd and Tony's grave on Memorial Day in East Hampton. Every year, we would bring American flags and flowers to put on the grave. Much to our surprise, we always found flowers already planted there. Puzzled, we couldn't think, who would be doing that, as we were the only relatives left in the area. However, one Memorial Day when we went there, we saw a woman planting flowers on Bernd's grave. Then we introduced ourselves, and the woman told us that her brother had been a close friend of Bernd's, but he had moved out of Connecticut years ago. Therefore, he had her promise to always plant flowers on Bernd's grave every Memorial Day. She always has, since then. We were amazed at her thoughtfulness and dedication. We feel, it says a great deal about Bernd, her brother, and most certainly herself.

Visiting Pointe Du Hoc

In May of 2004, two weeks before the 60th Anniversary of D-Day, Mona and I visited France. The first historic site, we went to was Pointe Du Hoc in Normandy, which I had planned to see, so many years before. Finally, there we were standing on the hallowed ground where sixty years ago, there had been a horrific battle fought by the Rangers, which resulted in terrible bloodshed and loss of life. We viewed the cliffs, which Tony and his fellow Rangers had climbed, and we saw the bombed out craters, which peppered the landscape.

We stood in the bunkers, where Tony and some of his fellow Rangers took cover while the U.S. Destroyers were shelling the area. We also viewed the Dagger Memorial Monument with the plaque below it, listing the names of all of the fallen Rangers. The monument had been built and placed on top of a German concrete bunker by the French government. It was dedicated to the 2nd Ranger Battalion for their heroic assault on Pointe Du Hoc. On January 11th, 1979, the ownership of the now historic thirteen acre battlefield was donated by the French Government to the United States.

It was a very moving experience, and I was thankful, to finally be there to see it. We also visited the various American museums, which were situated along the Normandy beach, where they exhibit memorabilia from the invasion on D-Day. While there, I mentioned to the workers in the various museums that my brother, Tony, was among the Rangers, who took part in the assault on Pointe Du Hoc. They were all very pleased to meet me, and told me that the

Rangers are regarded as heroes by the people of Normandy. There is also a museum in the area, which is dedicated exclusively to the brave men of the 2nd Ranger Battalion.

Our visit to Washington, D.C.

Several years ago, when I had taken Mona on her first trip to Washington, D.C., we visited the Vietnam Veterans Memorial. We noticed that people had left various items there, by the Wall of the Memorial. Some people left pictures and write-ups of their fallen loved ones, while others left flowers or various other items. On our first trip there, we didn't think of doing that. However, on our second trip there in September of 2006, we brought a little placard with Bernd's picture and a short write-up underneath it. Once we placed it by the Wall beneath his name, we saw a number of people bend down to read it. We were very pleased to see that. While we were there, Mona asked what was being done with the various items that are left by the Wall. She was told that, they are collected every week and placed in the archives of one of the government buildings. The hope being, that sometime in the future, there would be a museum where they could be displayed.

Then we visited the new World War II Memorial. It was very impressive and quite moving. There was also a small building on the grounds, which had informational brochures and a computer with a database registry listing the names of those, who served in World War II. While there, we were able to look up John and Tony's names.

Rose's Passing

One evening, while at home in North Carolina, Ronnie and her husband were watching television in their living room, when they both heard a noise. They thought the noise came from outside, so thinking that it was nothing to be alarmed about, they ignored it. Later, as Ronnie was walking into her bedroom to go to bed for the night, she looked in the foyer and noticed that a picture of our mother, which had been sitting on the table by the front door, was now lying face down. It looked as though, it had purposely been put that way. Then it occurred to her, that the picture falling down must have been the noise, which they had heard earlier. Fearing that, it was a bad omen and not wanting to give in to the fear, she told herself that, of course, everyone was fine, so she didn't call anyone. The next day, Rose's son, Kenny, called to say that Rose had suffered a cerebral hemorrhage. He went on to say, she had lost consciousness and was in the hospital. Ronnie was shaken and taken aback at the news. She realized then, that our mother's picture, which had fallen and been found lying face down, had indeed, been a message that something was truly wrong. Rose never regained consciousness. She passed away in the hospital a few days later, in October of 2006. She is buried alongside her husband, Richie, in St. Patrick's Cemetery in East Hampton, next to our mother.

'Ghost'

Throughout the years, it was usually during times of trouble that I smelled the scent of lilacs. Occasionally, Mona and I experienced the lilac scent, when everything was fine. It even occurred, a few times, during the course of writing this book.

In 2010, I had a strange and confirming experience. Once more, I smelled the scent of lilacs. This time, it was while I was watching the re-run of the movie called 'Ghost' on television. There was a scene in the movie, where Patrick Swayze was a spirit, trying to communicate with Demi Moore, but of course, she could not see him. While I was watching that scene, a tremendous scent of lilacs engulfed me, and it lasted a few minutes before dissipating. I believe that, it was my mother once again, trying to send me a message that she is here, even though, I can't see her, just like in the movie that I was watching.

Additional Sorrowful Losses

John's wife, Mary, died in 2006. Mary's husband, Al, died in 2007. Ronnie's second husband, Harry, died in 2011.

A Providential Find

One afternoon, while I was still in the process of writing this book my wife, Mona, decided to go shopping. A few hours after she was gone, she telephoned me and asked me for the name of the ship, which my family and I had come to America on. I thought that she knew the name, but apparently, she didn't. I told her the ship was called the 'Aquitania.' Then she went on, telling me about something peculiar, which had happened to her. Mona said, she had been out shopping, and she wanted to visit one more store, which she had never been to before, Antiques On Whitney in Hamden, but she decided to put it off as she was getting tired.

Instead, she decided to stop at a diner, which was right up the street from the antique shoppe and have a cup of coffee. While sitting there drinking her coffee, she had an urge to go to the shoppe, but thought she would go some other day as it was getting late, and she was still feeling tired. The urge continued, and Mona felt, she should go there. In a curious way, she felt, she was supposed to go there. She thought for certain, that there must be a reason for the strange and constant urging that she was experiencing. Therefore, she decided to give in to the unsettling feeling, so she went to the shoppe.

Upon entering the shoppe, one of the first things, which she noticed there was a beautiful old wooden carved picture of a ship with a brass nameplate, which read 'Aquitania.' It was then, she telephoned me. She asked Frank, the owner of the shoppe, what he knew about the picture. He replied that, he had purchased it from a man, who had inherited it from his grandmother, and that it had come from the family estate in the Cliff Walk section of Newport, Rhode Island. Frank said that, the picture had been in his shoppe for a few years. Mona finally realized that, the reason for the constant urging to visit the shoppe was because of that picture, being there in the shoppe.

When Mona told Frank, about some of my family's history and the constant urging feeling, which she experienced to visit his shoppe, he was surprised and thought that it was very strange. It was closing time, so I didn't have time to go there and view the picture. Therefore, Frank put a sign on the picture, holding it for us, until the following day. The next day, we went to the shoppe, and when I saw it, I thought it was beautiful. Here, was this carved picture of the ship, which brought me and my family to America. What's amazing about it is, when you look at the picture, it seems as if the ship is actually moving on the ocean water. We were thrilled and bought it. The picture is now hanging on the wall of my family room, where I gaze upon it daily and have the feeling, that I was meant to have it. I can't help, but wonder, was it some sort of a coincidence or truly an act of providence?

EPILOGUE

The saying is that, everyone has a story to tell, so that's my story. It's been quite an adventure and a long journey. It was a rough start, with many ups and downs, but the love of my mother and siblings was always present. Our faith in God and prayers gave us the hope and strength, which carried us through the difficult times. Then the widow's one overwhelming act of charity forever changed my life, the lives of my family, and those of our future generations.

Coming to America afforded us the opportunities to attain a better life, which wouldn't have been possible if we had remained in Czechoslovakia. Through hard work and perseverance, we were able to achieve success and happiness. All in all, life in America has been very good to us. We have tried to show our gratitude by doing our duty and serving in the armed forces in defense of our country. God Bless America!

REFERENCES

www.wikipedia.org (the free encyclopedia)

World War II

Battle of Guadacanal

Battle of the Russell Islands

Battle of New Georgia

Battle of New Guinea

Battle of the Northern Solomon Islands

Battle of the Philippines

Battle of Pointe Du Hoc

The Korean War

The Vietnam War

Battle of Khe Sanh

www.media.oaktreesys.com/abmc/pointeduhoc/popup.html (video)